VILLAGE
UNDER THE PLAIN

the story of Market Lavington

Bedeguar Books

The view towards the Hill from St Mary's Church tower, in the late 1920's.
Trees are where the Broadwell play area is now.
The picture was taken before Lavington Hill council estate and
'The Mead' extension to New Street (the Muddle) were built.

VILLAGE
UNDER THE PLAIN

the story of Market Lavington

Brian McGill

Village
Under The Plain
the story of Market Lavington

Copyright Brian McGill 1995

first published October 1995
by
Bedeguar Books
Warminster, Wiltshire

reprinted October 1997

Design and Layout
by
Danny Howell

Printed in Great Britain
by
Redwood Books
Trowbridge, Wiltshire

ISBN 1 872818 28 5

CONTENTS

INTRODUCTION

This is not a guide, but a history, and writing history involves making subjective choices. There may be too much here, for some, on the ancient village and not enough on the present one. There may be too much, for some, on long-forgotten issues of the 19th century and not enough on what seem issues today. There is not much folklore, no myth and very little which could be described as gossip. If you miss these things, blame history.

Village Under The Plain is dedicated to Peggy and Tom Gye, without whose help and encouragement it would not have been written. The photographs and illustrations have been loaned by Peggy from her personal albums, or reproduced from the Market Lavington Museum collection, where Peggy is, of course, not only the guiding light but also the Honorary Curator.

Especially helpful have been Pamela Slocombe, and Barbara and Robin Harvey of the Wiltshire Buildings Record. Preparation of the text for publication would not have been possible without the assistance of my daughter Annette McGill. Any factual or textual errors are, however, my own.

Brian McGill,
The Old House,
Market Lavington.
October 1995.

Beechwood and the bridge to 'the Grove,' circa 1905.
A favourite walk in former years.

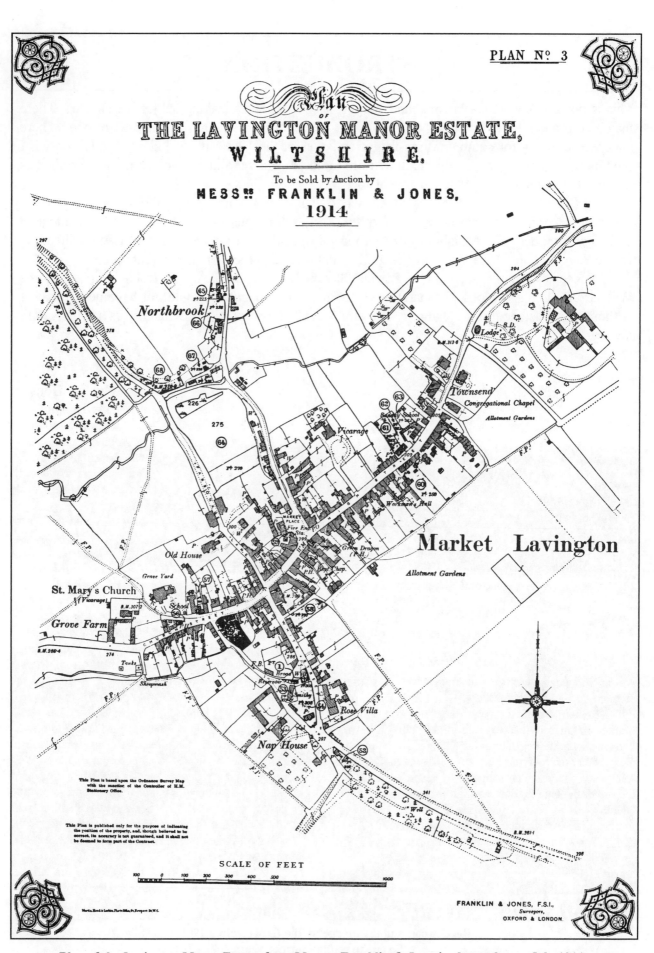

Plan of the Lavington Manor Estate, from Messrs. Franklin & Jones' sale catalogue, July 1914.

PREHISTORY TO THE PLAGUE

The Plain cuts across the southern skyline above Market Lavington. Its red brick and slate roofs and its grey, ancient church hugging the knoll, are typical of many Wiltshire villages which have grown north away from the slopes. They have been evolving since people first found and then settled on the tablelands and vales of this most ancient of counties. The early settlers built their sacred places on the high ground and in the valleys they grew their corn, as they do now, raised their flocks, as they also do now, and, after centuries, they became tribal. Did the tribe of a leader known as Laffa settle around the spring at Broadwell and Laffa's tun (town) become Lavington, or was it the tribe of the Leafings that built the tun or fort of the Leafings and so Lavynton? Later on the village became known as Stupellavynton, the Stupel or Staple being the post marking an ancient market, and finally it became the place of the market - Market Lavington. Stone Age, Iron Age, Saxons, Romans, Romano-British....... People have been forgetting their past here for thousands of years. What chance do we have now of rediscovering it?

Archaeology has recently given us that chance. It extended the history of Market Lavington by millennia, in 1990, with proof that humans had lived on and around the knoll north of the village High Street for at least 4,000 years. A dig on the Grove Farm housing estate, organised by Wessex Archaeology, revealed Neolithic and Bronze Age ditches, a Roman building about 1,650 years old and a pagan Anglo-Saxon cemetery dating back some 1,400 years.

The finds add to the rich store of knowledge of Wessex, where the landscape of ancient farm boundaries, villages, towns and cathedral cities fit so harmoniously with each other and into a pattern of valley, downland and plain. The growth of all these tells of the relationship between man and the land, and between man and his beliefs.

Ancient artefacts were found in and around Market Lavington in Victorian times, but little was known about the beginnings of village life before its mention in the *Doomsday Book* (1086). There had been some evidence to suggest an Anglo-Saxon building on the site of the church, and Norman masonry of an older church than St Mary's has been preserved, but these indications were fragmentary and inconclusive.

The Wessex Archaeology dig in June 1990 revealed prehistoric activity represented by two apparent boundary ditches and by worked flints and pottery. The flints showed that people were living and working in the area from the Mesolithic period - that is from about 3,000 BC. One of the ditches contained charcoal linked with worked flint, suggesting occupation during the Neolithic or more possibly the Early Bronze Age.

From a much later time they found one small Roman building, but the artefacts recovered suggest that there were many others nearby. The discoveries also point to a south and south-eastwards extension of the Roman settlement into the modern village, indicating that the excavated area lay on the northern periphery of what might have been an extensive and yet undefined Roman settlement. The dating evidence provided by the pottery suggests that the occupation spanned the whole Roman period, but most of the material recovered dates to the late third and fourth centuries, when Romans were already becoming Romano-British.

The majority of the excavated artefacts were early to middle Saxon and the site showed there was a settlement, a cemetery and an earthwork. Settlement of the site after the Saxon period was clear. The archaeologists identified two buildings as well as a number of north-south ditches from the early medieval period. The later medieval and post-medieval periods were not noticeable, suggesting to the archaeologists that with the development of the borough after 1248 there was a shift in focus from the area around the church towards a market place to the east. That market place gave Market Lavington its name.

The present-day village at the foot of the north-west edge of Salisbury Plain covered 4,721 acres 300 years ago. Until the 19th century, Lavington comprised three detached pieces - Market Lavington, including the church and the village, the tithing of Easterton and the tithing of Gore. The parish of Market Lavington was, and to some extent remains, a curious shape in that it is about five miles long, running north to south and less than a mile wide. Easterton was a similar shape, though smaller in area, and it was separated from Market Lavington by Fiddington, a detached portion of the parish of West Lavington. Gore was a triangular plot of land nearly a mile southwest of Market Lavington and separated from it by lands in West Lavington. After 1874 Easterton was reinstituted as a new ecclesiastical and civil parish. In 1884 Gore become part of West Lavington and at the same time Fiddington became part of Market Lavington. The modern parish covers 3,806 acres, but about half of this area is on the chalk uplands of the Plain and is occupied by the Army. Access is possible only when the Army is not engaged in artillery practice or manoeuvres.

The northern part of the parish is on clay at about 250 feet above sea level, and from the clay the land rises to a ridge 300 feet high on Ledge Hill. Between Ledge Hill and the northern boundary of the parish lay the common meadows, which were enclosed in the 17th century. Most of the village is built on greensand which in turn lies on clay, and the moisture which reaches the greensand is held there by the impervious clay. The bonus for Market Lavington is that it has a well-drained soil to retain its well water and springs. Above the upper greensand levels is chalk, in three distinct layers. The lowest level, rich in soluble clay and known as "the Clays," is along the southern edge of the village proper. Above the Clays, the ridge area is still known as the Sands and it too was largely common land until it was enclosed. The portion that remained as East Lavington Common was the site of several small orchards in the 18th century and in more recent times some of the land was reserved for parish allotments.

The first settlements at Market Lavington were linked to the ancient ridge-way road running along the northern edge of Salisbury Plain within half a mile of the village. The ridge road was a field boundary by 1225 and for much longer it has carried traffic from Westbury below the Plain to Pewsey. The early track was formed by a band of very hard chalk known as Melbour Rock and many small quarries used it over the years to build roads. From the ridge the land falls southwards to a stream fed by several springs that rises in Easterton and flows westward past Northbrook and Lady Wood Meads to Russell Mill. There it joins another stream rising in West Lavington and the two streams form the western boundary of the parish. On the southern edge of the village a spring, Broadwell, was a main source of water for villagers until 1936. In Market Lavington the land running north to south rises slightly as it approaches the village High Street. Then the terrain becomes steeper, sweeping up to the heights of Lavington Hill which, at 600 feet, forms the edge of Salisbury Plain. Here, on the upland part of the parish, flocks of sheep grazed for thousands of years and provided the fleeces for the village's oldest craft - weaving. There were four or five farm-houses in this upland half of the parish before the first War Department acquisitions in 1897. These are now gone and there is restricted agricultural use for some 2,000 acres.

Crossing the ancient ridge road is the old road from Devizes to Salisbury. It enters the parish at Dewey's Water, on the northern boundary, passes through the village via Parsonage Lane and continues through White Street and up Lavington Hill to the Plain and Salisbury some 17 miles to the south. About half of the road has passed over British Army firing ranges for the past century and is usually closed to civilian traffic.

THE NEOLITHIC PERIOD

Evidence of Neolithic settlement at Market Lavington was fragmentary before the 1990 excavations, though the area is rich in prehistoric sites. Dating of the sites on the knoll around the Parish Church must be speculative. It is known only that the hunter-gatherers who travelled freely from Europe to Britain in the warming climate after 6,000 BC began to clear forests and to farm during the next millennium. By 4,000 BC new immigrants of a Mediterranean type had brought cereal seeds, domesticated cattle, sheep, and tools for cultivation and more extended settlement to form what we now regard as the Neolithic or New Stone Age culture.

Present knowledge of this culture in Wessex locates it on the Marlborough Downs, on the western edge of Salisbury Plain, on the Plain west of the Avon, and in Cranborne Chase. These Neolithic people had a cultural and tribal cohesion as is shown by their building of enclosures interrupted by ditches that have come to be called causeway camps. The function of these enclosures is unclear, but at least initially they were for tribal gatherings. In Wiltshire five large ones have been identified at Windmill Hill, near Avebury, at Knapp Hill on the north side of the Pewsey Vale, some 15 kilometres from Market Lavington, near Stonehenge and at Whitesheet Hill, north of Mere. The largest, at Windmill Hill, was 21 acres in size. The Neolithic settlement at Market Lavington was probably too small to have a ceremonial use, but the dig did reveal indications of an enclosure, which might have had the more practical use of a fortification. The five largest enclosures in Wessex appear to have been converted to forts in the third to second millennia BC when drier weather decreased food stocks and there was concern about marauding foreigners.

There is no evidence of Neolithic burial at Market Lavington, though the intense use of the site over so long a period may have erased the earlier tombs, but there is ample evidence that the site was occupied in prehistoric times. Flints have been unearthed at Grove Farm, and in the garden of 9 Parsonage Lane an amateur archaeologist discovered a fine flint arrow-head. The Grove Farm site's chief prehistoric features are two ditches (probably boundaries) and one of these contains a charcoal deposit in association with worked flints, which probably date from the Early Bronze Age (1,500 BC).

On the less-settled hillsides within a few kilometres of the settlement the standard Neolithic burial practices appear in the shape of the long and round barrows typical of burials before and after 3,000 BC. There are two large barrows close together, a third of a mile south of Cadley Farm and a quarter of a mile east of Freith Farm and close to the north side of Rowbery Lane. Archaeologists opened the barrow on Freith Farm in 1924. It had been much damaged by ploughing, but the dig discovered the primary burial five and a half feet beneath the surface. It consisted of a cinerary urn nine inches high, buried upright, and containing burnt bones. The urn appeared to be resting on a funerary pyre and the bones had been put in the urn after the burning. Two other cremated burials, without urns, were found in the mound above the primary burial. The mound also held a finely-worked

A harvest scene, looking towards Easterton from Fiddington Hill.

The Grove in 1930. St Mary's and the Old House in the distance.

Church Street in 1850, from a water colour by Owen Carter.
Nos.18 and 20 are on the immediate left.

An early sketch of the bridge into the village from West Lavington, with Cornbury Mill in the background.
The stream at this point forms part of the parish boundary.

leaf-shaped arrowhead, Bronze Age pottery and flint flakes. There are several more barrows near Tilshead, including one long barrow which measures 130 metres. We must presume links between the Market Lavington settlement and the Neolithic purely-religious centres at Avebury and Stonehenge.

The gradual decline of the so-called Wessex Culture came with the new Iron Age and an influx of Celtic immigrants who had a lively trade with the Continent. The new settlers built farmsteads and fenced them, thus laying down land-division and boundaries which, as in the Market Lavington settlement, formed the basis of parish boundaries 2,000 years later. The Celtic field systems have been absorbed into Lavington's village structure but they can be seen clearly at Fyfield Down, near Marlborough, simply because later settlement has not incorporated them.

The period after 400 BC was marked by increasing Celtic immigration and local unrest. Small forts became numerous and a division grew between the people of north-east and south-west Wiltshire. The division ran roughly along the line of the Salisbury Avon and Wylye rivers. The fortifications, especially along the Wylye, became complex - and intimidating.

THE ROMANS

Roman settlements in Wiltshire followed decades of unrest and conquest. Claudius's invasion in 43 AD was far away, to the east, but eventually the hostile Durotriges and other clans in the West became too great a threat to be ignored. The Roman general and later emperor, Vespasian, took the Second Legion across the south-west, through Salisbury, to destroy fortresses on Maiden Castle and Hod Hill, and his army occupied Exeter. The Romans secured the silver and lead mines in the Mendips and began the building of the great Fosse Way, linking Bath to Lincoln.

The growth of Roman-controlled and Roman-named towns in Wiltshire - Verlucio (the present-day Sandy Lane) and Sorviodunum (Salisbury) brought in their wake large country estates and country houses or villas, but settlements were sparse on Salisbury Plain. Only two villa sites have been found locally, at Pit Meads, near Sutton Veny, and at Netheravon. The area was probably treated as an imperial estate supplying grain direct to the Roman army or to overseas-based traders. The indigenous people were thus denied the land and the product from the land that would have made them rich enough to build on a comparatively grand scale. So the majority of the population lived in hamlets or small towns, and it is into this category that the Market Lavington settlement falls. These villages or hamlets had none of the formal planning of the classic Roman town or fort, but they soon adopted the larger field layouts to replace the small square field boundaries of the Celtic occupation.

The Market Lavington site certainly had room for these larger fields and the output from these may have provided some villagers with sufficient status to build grander housing. The archaeological excavation unearthed box flue tiles on and near the hill crest and these suggested that some of the Roman buildings may have been important. Expert opinion is that Market Lavington's Parish Church, St Mary's, may stand on the site of a Norman or even a Saxon one. Roman pottery shards, remnants of heating flues, and coinage have been found around Market Lavington over the years but human remains from the Roman period are comparatively rare. In Easterton, in 1931, workmen found a Roman burial in a wooden coffin, five feet deep, while digging to extend drainage. In the coffin with the skeleton were two small pots of New Forest pottery. The burial was at the end of the garden of the house now built close to and on the opposite side of the road from the house known as The Kestrels. The pottery is now at Devizes Museum.

There are subtle signs that by the 3rd century AD Roman occupation in the downlands was in decline. Large tracts of arable land on Salisbury Plain were being converted to sheep-walks, and Roman settlements, such as they were, were shrinking in the upland villages, including the hamlet which was to become Market Lavington. From the 4th century the changes were accelerated and "Barbarian" raids brought destruction to many villas. Near the end of the century legions were withdrawn to the continent to quell troubles there and local anarchy grew. The so-called Dark Ages were beginning.

THE SAXONS

The Saxon settlement and burials at Market Lavington coincide approximately with the 6th century Battle of Badon where the legendary Arthur, leader of the Britons, won a famous, though not conclusive, victory. Contemporary records of the Saxon invasion and early settlements are minuscule and suspect. Gildas, a Christian monk who died in 572 AD, speaks of "fierce Saxons admitted into the island like so many wolves into the fold." Other monks recorded the Badon battle no less than three centuries later, so this too may have legendary aspects. The most detailed account of this dim period comes from the *Anglo-Saxon Chronicle*, a record in Old English which is, however, even further removed from the events it records as it dates from 1154. This account says that two invading Saxon leaders, Cerdic and Cynric, occupied "the West Saxons' kingdom," probably based on Winchester, in 519. They defeated a British force in 552 at Old Sarum and in 556 Cynric defeated another British force at Barbury Castle, near Swindon. The size of the forces involved in these engagements put them in perspective. The original invasion of the two leaders was in five ships with probably no more than 250 men, constituting in those days a formidable army. Cynric's son, Ceawlin, was victorious at first but he suffered a defeat near "Adam's Grave," a prominent chambered long barrow on the

From a water colour by Owen Carter in 1850. The main building in the centre, now drastically altered, is currently the Co-op Stores. The right hand end, since demolished, was a 'Market House' on oak pillars. Obviously of very early date are the elaborate barge boards. To the right of the building the stocks can be seen and also a building which was possibly a lock-up before it housed the horsedrawn fire engine.
It is interesting to note how the road level has been raised in the interim.

An early drawing of the Parsonage, formerly in Parsonage Lane, from Rev. Atley's book of 1850. The house was demolished because it was supposed to be haunted. Nos.6 and 8 now occupy the site.

north side of Pewsey Vale and lost his kingdom.

The Market Lavington Saxon settlement and cemetery, with its warriors buried beside their weapons, recalls this turbulent century. Within the settlement two sunken-featured buildings and a portion of a possible hall (timbered halls were known to the Saxons) have been identified. The great quantity of Saxon pottery recovered spans the whole Saxon period: Early, Middle and Late.

The settlement area lies immediately to the west of a large linear early Saxon earthwork and probably spread over St Mary's churchyard and east along the ridge which now forms the garden of the Old House. If the Saxons did find the remains of Roman buildings on the brow of the hill they most certainly would have used the materials for their own rebuilding.

The cemetery appears to have been large and the 42 individual graves unearthed do not give a true indication of its size. The burials lay to the west of the settlement, and human remains uncovered in the 1930's and in 1986, still further west, suggest the cemetery must have covered an area of at least 180 by 150 metres.

All the burials were pagan. One adult shows a sword-cut severing an upper right arm; the severed arm having been placed in the grave in almost the correct position. Another adult shows an iron arrowhead lodged through the skull. Iron knives are buried with both males and females, and several varieties of beads are all associated with female burials. One skeleton was of a man two metres in height, making him a giant among his contemporaries. It appears he died of syphilis. Sufficient wood remained of some spears to identify it as either cherry or maple.

One woman is buried with a gilded copper alloy saucer brooch, 32 amber beads, numerous fragmentary blue glass beads, ten dark blue or purple glass beads, an iron knife and some iron nails, the latter suggesting a coffin.

Another female is buried with an iron buckle, iron knife, amber bead and two glass beads. Another woman had with her a copper alloy brooch, an iron blade, two iron knife blades, an amber bead, four pottery sherds, an early Mid-Saxon pottery sherd and one early Romano-British bead rimmed pottery sherd. Another had a complete Saxon pot, two copper alloy pins, an unidentified iron object, four iron fragments, charcoal, a pottery sherd, an ivory or chalk bead, seven glass beads and no less than 58 amber beads.

One adult male's funerary objects suggest a warrior. There is a spearhead by his left shoulder, a shield-boss, a second spearhead, and an iron knife. There are only four child burials. One has a glass bead and some iron fragments, while another has an iron knife and a nail. One warrior lay with a large whetstone, which was probably used for sharpening spears or swords.

A large quantity of animal bones was recovered from the site. More than half of these were from cattle, nearly 30 per cent from goats, 12 per cent from pigs and less than two per cent from horses. There were, however, bones from dogs, cats, a rabbit, possibly a mole, fowl, geese, and red, roe and fallow deer. Archaeologists are convinced that the Market Lavington Saxons were prosperous and of a higher social status than many of their contemporaries. An indicator of this is the presence of the horse bones. Horses were much prized and few communities could afford them.

CHRISTIANITY AND ALFRED

We will never know when the Market Lavington pagan Saxons converted to Christianity, but in 635 Birinus, a Benedictine monk from Rome, baptised a Saxon leader, Cynegils, at Dorchester in Oxfordshire; and King Ine, who came to the throne in 688, fostered religious houses at Glastonbury and Malmesbury.

The land these Christian Saxons had inherited was beautiful but as severe as the heath and sand dunes of Jutland and Frisia, which they left, or the Baltic forests which they had raided. It was not the England we know or even the England Chaucer knew 700 years ago. Cold and storm are the themes which run through the earliest English poetry, and the bards sang of brown bears, wild cattle and wolves roaming the forests. Men hunted wild boar within ten miles of London, and eagles sailed over the fens. English rivers were undrained and opened into great estuaries as they neared the sea.

In Somerset the Tone and Parret marsh made a huge no-man's land from Glastonbury to Athelney and "the immovable pillar of the West Saxons," King Alfred, knew and used this no-man's land when the heathen Vikings or Danes, as we call them, began their raids along the south coast and up into Wessex in the 8th century. England was reeling from the attacks of Ubbi and Ivar The Boneless, he of the raven banner, and York and Northumbria were in ruins when Alfred decided to fight. At first, after the winter of 870-71, the Danes pushed the Saxon English back to Hampshire, Savernake Forest and onto Salisbury Plain, and by Easter 878, Alfred was hiding in the Somerset marshes. The change in his fortunes came suddenly and probably because the Danes were divided. He defeated armies at Wareham and Exeter and should have completed the rout at Gloucester. The Danes escaped and Alfred rallied his forces in Wiltshire, east Hampshire and Somerset. The Saxons, or as we regard them now, the English, met the Danes at Mere. Controversy surrounds the site of the next and decisive great battle. We know it was fought at a hamlet called Edington, but scholars are uncertain about which Edington. Most favoured is the one seven miles from Market Lavington, where the majority opinion says Alfred won a famous victory commemorated, possibly, by an earlier version of the white horse carved above Bratton. His chief opponent,

Guthrum, swore at the treaty of Wedmore to evacuate Wessex and to be baptised, and he kept his word.

Alfred learned from his victory. His 1,000 or so Wessex farmers which had defied the professional armies of the Danes were dispersed, so he organised a force of mounted thegns and planned and instituted a system of fortified towns across Wessex, known as burhs. The stress was on commercial enterprise as well as fortification, and the burhs were soon minting their own coins and establishing markets. Among these were Tilshead, Warminster, Marlborough, Calne and Bradford on Avon. Armed and mounted men patrolled the old road across Salisbury Plain and carried the King's word to the hamlets. These hamlets were soon to become villages and the villages were soon to become towns.

One of these hamlets was at the foot of the old Plain road heading north and crossing a stream frequented by itinerant shepherds. Huddled around the stream were a few farms and while Alfred's heirs fought the Danes the farmers saw the usefulness of a loose communal structure. The pre-historic settlement, which had become a Roman one, was re-born as a Saxon village, soon to be the medieval Lavington.

AFTER DOOMSDAY

That early community probably heard nothing of the coronation of Alfred's great grandson, Edgar, in Bath during 973 and it is probably just as well because the peace promised by a coronation uniting England under one Saxon ruler was short-lived. The Danes returned and their raiding coincided with the 38-year reign of the well-named Ethelred the Unready. Saxon England fell into ruin and a Dane, Canute, and his kinsmen reigned - and, inevitably, plotted against each other. The death of Canute's step-son, Edward the Confessor, in 1066 brought Harold his brief rule before it was ended at Hastings by the bowmen of Duke William of Normandy - "the Conqueror."

Before the Norman conquest an estate in Lavington was held by Edward's Queen, Edith, who died in 1075. The village achieved its first written historic mention in the 11th century as "Laventone," and its status was that of a manor. William the Conqueror's 1086 tally of his domains in the *Doomsday Book* notes that Robert the Marshal, presumably a close supporter of William, held the manor, presumably after Queen Edith's death. Lavington's area was 15 hides (a hide being a variable measure, usually reckoned to be 120 acres). In Lavington, half this total area of 1,800 acres was worked for the lord of the manor by seven slaves using four ploughs. There were in addition 14 villeins or bondmen and 14 smallholders with five ploughs. There were two mills paying 16 shillings and fourpence to the lord, 20 acres of meadow, 12 acres of

woodland and a large pasture area. The annual income from the manor was £20, making it of medium size.

So here we have the nucleus of a village community, a development from the life-style of those early settlers, the people of Laffa or the Leafings, who had lived in proximity to each other for safety or convenience. This nucleus saw the potential of the spring in the south and the fresh water in the north and its members owned and tilled the undulating land north of the Plain. All of Wiltshire had no more than 50,000 people in 1086, making it, nevertheless, the tenth most populous in England. It had ten boroughs, with the old Saxon centre of Tilshead the focus of sheep-raising in the centre of the downs as it had been for centuries. These fortified boroughs - Market Lavington being part of the Devizes borough - formed the basis of local government. In each borough there was a mint, a market, and sometimes a local court. Within the boroughs were the "Hundreds," each of these consisting of a hundred hides, or 12,000 acres. The Hundreds were on the lowest rung of the State's jurisdiction. Market Lavington was in the Swanborough hundred. By 1100 AD the counties of southern England had taken shape and in each a Royal shire-reeve (sheriff) collected revenue.

In the century after its mention in the *Doomsday Book*, Market Lavington was to suffer, as did the whole of Wiltshire, from the civil war which grew out of a State-Church confrontation. King Stephen (1135-1154) issued two charters of liberties confirming his alliance with the Church, but his clerical opponents recognised his lack of resolution and soon they were urging the great barons to demand extortionate concessions. Stephen rounded on Roger of Salisbury and the bishops of Ely and Lincoln when these three and others demanded that neither their goods nor their persons should be subject to secular jurisdiction. The king seized their castles and the clergy as a body declared against him and England, and especially Wiltshire, experienced unprecedented anarchy.[1] Stephen, a poor general, found himself besieging or being besieged in castles and forts across the land. Devizes Castle, rebuilt by Bishop Roger, was taken and retaken five times, Malmesbury was taken twice and Marlborough once. Salisbury and Trowbridge castles held out against sieges, but Wilton surrendered and the loss of human life was high when humans were few.

THE MEDIEVAL VILLAGE

So as Wiltshire entered the 13th century a quarter of the county was described as a waste-land and the peasants suffered from inflation and falling wages in an economy that was always striving to survive with some small degree of security. The economic core of feudal society was by now the village community, usually called the

---

[1] "Men said openly that Christ and His saints slept; such things, and more than we can say, did we endure nineteen winters for our sins," said an early chronicler.

Harvesting at Lock's Sands, Northbrook, circa 1914.
The crop was probably potatoes. The bearded gentleman is Francis Pinchin.

East Clay, looking eastwards, circa 1912.

A view from St Mary's Church tower, circa 1909. In the foreground is the Old School House, built for the headmaster; now the village Museum. On the left is the Old House and its magnificent cedar.

Broadwell, source of drinking water for many residents over the centuries, showing three dipping wells and a pump. Mains water came in 1936. The photo is taken from the footbridge. Trees occupy what is now the Play Area. One lad has secured a vantage point on the pump.

manor. In its origin the manor was a piece of land, but in its economic and political sense it meant a freehold estate, held ultimately from the King in return for rent and service. It was divided into the demesne, farmed directly for the benefit of the lord using his tenants' services, and the tenants' holdings. The tenants could be freemen, owing only a chief rent to the lord, or customary tenants who were bondmen owing services and/or rent. The lord's steward took the manor courts twice a year. These covered not only misdemeanors but also elected officers from among the tenantry. The jury at the court was drawn from tenants. The lord's chief official below the steward was the bailiff, but the man who had the day-to-day running of the estate was the reeve, chosen annually by the bondmen from among their number. So in practise the manor could be an administrative or judicial centre for one large settlement or for a number of scattered hamlets. The chief virtue of the system was its self-sufficiency.

In the neighbourhood of Market Lavington there were the Norman landowners in the settlements north of the Plain - William son of Maurice, Master Robert, and Geoffrey son of Simon, and Geoffrey Grangia (Grange), Ralph le Vader, Walter Messager, Robert de Mara (later the Delameres) and the Rokellas (later the Rochelles). There were solid Anglo-Saxon names there too, though often with French trimmings. There was John de la Feythe (who owned Frieth Farm, north of Lavington, in 1286), John atte Grove, who was "at" Grove Farm in 1327, and Roger de Northebrok, (Northbrook) in 1282. We also have Adam de Essesse (Adam of Essex), Richard Moryn (Morin), Adam de Spineto (Adam Spinney), Simon de Fonte (Simon Wells), Robert and William Umfray (the Humphreys), Ralph de Wike (Ralph Wick), William Coterel, William Prepositus (William Reeve), John Bubulcus (John Ploughman) and also Robert Carpentarius (Robert Carpenter).

There are two prime sources for the development of Market Lavington in the post Conquest period. The archaeological investigations connected with the Grove Farm estate in 1990-91 showed that in the late 12th century there was a shift in the focus of the village from the ancient Saxon settlement on the brow of the hill running east-west to High Street and Church Street, though some building activity continued along Parsonage Lane during the late 12th century. The town re-organisation may have coincided with the 12th century reconstruction of St Mary's Church, which is certainly Norman in origin and may well have Saxon foundations.

The other source for the village's development in this period is the legal document of Lavington land transfers recorded in the Edington Cartulary, or estate registry, now in the British Museum, though this does not contain a map and probably none existed at the time. The Cartulary is an illuminated manuscript written in Latin and accessible only to those few, other than churchmen, who were likely to have any knowledge of the language. Some among even the nobility were unable to read or write and the vocabulary of the nobles and commoners alike was compounded of the three tongues - English (itself a Saxon dialect with some Celtic borrowings), French and Latin.[2] Legal conservatism kept French as a professional language for another 200 years, but a statute of 1362 ordered that in all law courts men should plead in their mother tongue, while the Chancellor of England kept the records of his court in English. Even by the 16th century the authorities were struggling to describe with the written word property which would be recognisable by others than those who owned it or lived on it. We have such a document on the manor of Easterton Gernon, adjoining Market Lavington, thanks to the Duchy of Lancaster's Survey of Manors, dated 1591.[3]

Returning to an earlier Lavington, in the 12th, 13th and 14th centuries, the cultivated land on the manor of Lavington was typical of thousands of others in southern England. It was divided into three large fields of several hundred acres each. The cultivated arable fields, as distinct from the uncultivated meadow land, were subdivided into a number of rectangular acre or half-acre strips and these were divided from each other by little mounds or balks of unploughed earth. There were no hedges - hence the use of the phrase "the open-field system." The acre strips were grouped

---

[2] Edward II took his coronation oath in 1307 not in English but in French.

[3] Part of this document reads (spelling modernised): "The boundary on the north part thereof at a meadow called the King's Croftes, from thence eastward by Flower's Hedge to Newman's Corner, thence southward as the mere leads, dividing this manor and Eastcott to Foot Burrow, and thence continuing the same mere southward to Easterton Coomes, being the utmost point on the south; therehence westward following the balles and markes which divide this Manor and Fydington to Green Cliff, and so thence northward by the mere stones to Red land, wherehence to the western point of Court Close, from thence northward as the hedge leads to the western edge of Easterton Sand, and so thence following the hedges to the western side of Twenty Acres, and thence continuing the hedge northward to the south point of Potterne Park, and from thence following the hedges eastward into King's Croft aforesaid, where it began." The survey adds, as was the custom, that within these boundaries "all waifs, strays, felons, goods, etc., and all other things incident to a royalty do belong to Her Majesty." The lord of the manor of Easterton Gernon in 1591 was Walter Fisher and the freeholders, as opposed to tenants, were Robert Bishop, Christian Sainsbury (an early appearance of a name still well known in the area), Thomas Kill and William Kill.

together in bunches of ten or twelve, known as shots. Strips cut short by meeting some obstacle like a track or boundary were called butts, and irregularly-shaped corners of land that could not be shaped properly in strips were known as gores. This is the origin of the name of one portion of the Market Lavington manor, St John a' Gore, which was an unshaped piece of meadow.

The social structure centred on the manorial system, with the lord of the manor at its head. The social status of this lord varied widely, though all manorial lords were answerable to the monarch. He or she might be immensely powerful and, on occasion, have more wealth and power than the monarch. He might also be no more than a knight who had earned favour through feats of arms or merely loyalty. At the lower end of the scale he might be comparatively poor and certainly by the 14th century simple knights grew steadily poorer as a result of the crippling taxes which paid for the splendours of court and the horrors of war. Instances exist of knights turning to banditry to support themselves.[4]

The lord of the manor's income came from produce on land he owned directly or from land he leased out - a leasing arrangement, incidentally, which was to continue with few significant changes until the end of the 19th century. His tenants could be either "free", villeins or slaves. The "free" tenants were few in number. Mostly they paid rent and not labour-in-kind and unlike all others on the manor, except of course the lord, they had security of tenure. Any attempt to remove this class of tenant could result in an appeal against the lord to the royal courts of justice. By far the largest group of tenants were the villeins. These paid their rent in kind - with hens at Christmas, eggs at Easter, and in money. The villein's main liability was, however, the obligation to work for his lord - two or three days a week all the year round or boon-work, at harvest and seed time. The villein also paid to the lord a heriot, usually the best animal on his holding, when he succeeded his father and he could not leave the manor without the lord's permission. He was nevertheless allowed to accumulate private property which he might use to buy his freedom and he could sit on juries and serve in the army. The slaves were few in number after the Norman conquest.

Usually the free tenants or villeins held about 30 acres, though these were not grouped together to form a compact block, but scattered throughout the three fields of the manor. This may sound inconvenient, impractical and even absurd to us, but its primary motive was the desire for equality and the concept also fitted in well with the co-operative system of cultivation pursued on the manor. The tenant farming his 30 acres had to

combine with his neighbours to make up a complete plough team of six or eight oxen and with this team he and his neighbours ploughed the land jointly.

The lord's share of the land was made up in the same way as that of the peasants, only in his case the scattered strips amounted to about a third or a half of the whole cultivated area. This was known as the lord's demesne or domain, in contrast to the tenants' share which were called the land in villeinage. The demesne land was tilled by the labour services of the tenants and the lord had the right to graze waste-land and bring it under the plough and put the tenants to work on the new holdings.

The chief crops raised in Wiltshire were wheat, rye, barley, oats, peas, beans and vetches. Market Lavington farmers had to cart their produce, especially corn, to Devizes and further afield by packhorse over roads which were little more than dirt tracks and these were often impassable in winter and wet weather. The land south of the village and embracing the edge of Salisbury Plain formed three farming regions. On the Clays lay the best arable land and farmers said that the soil was so rich there were no fallow fields. Across the top of the Clays ran the ridge road, which formed a rough boundary between the Lower and Middle Chalk. The area of the Middle Chalk was known as "the Hill" and above the Hill came the sheep downs on the Upper Chalk. The yields were not large, partly because much land was put under the plough which was better suited for grazing. The animals reared were mainly oxen, sheep and pigs. Oxen were considered superior to horses in medieval times for pulling the plough. Cattle were valued for their milk or for ploughing and sheep for their wool. Bacon was the only flesh meat eaten regularly by the working classes. The greatest problem for the farmer was keeping animals alive during the winter. The only winter fodder available was hay and this was never sufficient, so large-scale slaughter of surplus animals had to be carried out in the autumn and the flesh preserved in brine. Salt was expensive and one of the causes of leprosy during the Middle Ages was the eating of meat which had been insufficiently salted and had begun to decay.

All in all, life at nearly every level was unimaginably hard. The villein ate badly, his clothes were basic and his two-roomed accommodation which he often shared with his animals, was damp and often freezing. Naturally he felt exploited by his lord, his lord's staff and even by his religious mentor, the parson. To add to his miseries there was the manorial court, which met twice a year and which spent much of its time making sure the common folk toed the line drawn by custom.

---

[4] The King was ruthless in his demands from his knights for money to pay for foreign wars or court extravagances. He levied fines in lieu of their service and on occasion ordered that those who had not obeyed an order to fight or pay their fine should appear before his council. The fines often went to pay the wages of foreign mercenaries in European campaigns.

THE ROCHELLES AND THE DELAMERES

By the 12th century two families, one certainly Norman, were in possession of the manor of Lavington - the Rokeleys or Rochelles and the Norman de la Maras or Delameres. Four sons of a de la Mara came to England from their ancestral home in la Mare in Autretot, Normandy, in the 11th century and they settled in several counties in southern England. Branches of them owned property in Essex, Gloucestershire, Hereford, Oxfordshire and Somerset as well as Wiltshire; and the name survives in Fisherton Delamere, in the vale of Wylye, and in Leigh Delamere, near Chippenham.

In Somerset the Delameres left their most enduring mark at Nunney, formerly Nunney Delamere, near Frome. The moated ruins of their castle, built by Sir John Delamere in the latter third of the 14th century, still remain, evoking, as no words can, the way the minor manorial lords lived. The structure, enclosed by four towers, had provision for four floors, with massive fireplaces in each floor, sharing common flues as they rise higher. In those warlike times many of the window embrasures are no more than firing positions for archers, and interior lighting even in daylight must have been limited. Staff worked and probably slept in the ground floor on rush matting. The great hall - modest in dimensions compared with many - was on the next floor and here the manorial lord and friends ate and made merry - on rush matting nevertheless. The lord and his family slept on the next floor - well laid with rush matting. Overall, floor space was not large, remembering that provision had to be made for visitors, servants and more warlike retainers.

The tombs of the Delameres of Nunney are in Nunney's Parish Church. Two couples, the knights carved in pale stone and shown in full armour, lie in a window embrasure to which they were shifted from a prominent position in the church. One knight has a lion at his feet and under his head a mantle and a leopard's head. Perhaps one of these was a Lavington Delamere of a later generation.

The Delameres appear to have owned the entire Lavington manor by the middle of the 12th century and

Godfrey Rochelle arrived in the parish no later than 1134, possibly as a tenant of the Delameres. The origin of the Rochelles is unclear, though there were Rokeleys in Kent, Essex and Suffolk in the 13th century. In Market Lavington their fortunes improved with the decision by the Delameres to sell them half the manor. Joint ownership of a manor was not unusual in these early centuries and, as we have seen in the case of the Delameres, it was also common for a knight's interests to extend to more than one property and occupation.[5]

The heads of the two families held the manor by service to the Crown, as had become common in the wake of the Conquest. Service was castle guard-duty at Devizes for 40 days in time of war or an annual rent of 20 shillings in peace-time,[6] and neither lord dared challenge that service. What they did challenge was each other's right to a half share and the joint owners deemed it necessary to draw up a document showing their division of the property, with Godfrey's grandson, William Rochelle, holding one portion and Peter Delamere's son holding the other. This was not, however, an end to disputes over the property.

The families' most forthright round of confrontation about the division of the manor came in 1220 in the King's Court,[7] when William, son of the William who had acquired the manor from the Delameres, claimed sole rights to the manor. Peter Delamere responded with a similar claim and a formal partitioning recognising that both had rights to the property came in 1225, though not before the two knights had resorted to "a wager of battle," in which William Rochelle was the plaintiff and Peter Delamere the defendant. From the Cartulary list it does appear that Delamere won the "battle," which actually involved a physical, though non-lethal, fight. The robed judges of the King's Court presided over the contest, which was fought by substitutes, or "champions." The champions wielded a staff, measuring 45 inches in length, and a leather shield. The fight continued until one contestant cried "craven" or the stars appeared. If night fell and there was no result, the defendant was the winner, and this may have happened in Lavington's case as Peter Delamere, the defendant, was adjudged to

---

[5] ".......The knights who came to England with William the Conqueror were primarily soldiers upon whom the king could call, but they soon became landowners and, eventually, administrators. The knight, as lord of his little domain, became the dispenser of justice and keeper of the peace within the framework of the manor court.

[6] In the 13th century there were an estimated 1,500 knights among England's estimated population of some two and a half million. As many of the 1,500 were knights attached to the Royal household, perhaps only 1,200 were in the shires. In the shires themselves some knights were "girded with the sword," indicating leaders in society, involved in local administration and able to raise household troops.

[7] The King's Court of Westminster was superior to the more ancient Hundred Court, which sat monthly and dealt with minor cases. In the shire, the Royal representative, the Sheriff, held a court twice yearly in each hundred at which the main business was the proper working of the parish. On the manor there were held two courts: the Court Leet, dealing with theft, assaults and market and trade offences, and the Court Baron, for civil cases such as ownership of land. A Court Baron was held as late as the 19th century in Market Lavington.

The stream at Northbrook, looking westward from the bridge. The stream bed was once used by horsedrawn wagons and carts coming from the Market Place towards Parsonage Lane - an early 'one-way' system.

have won.

A court document showing how the manor was split between them, recorded in the Edington Cartulary, gives us more than just field and family names. In describing the way in which the property was to be split up it provides invaluable information about precisely what existed in "the township" of Market Lavington more than seven hundred years ago. This "entire town" consisted of "the living of the church there, the messuage [in effect a property, usually a building and land] which belonged to William Rochelle and "the moiety [portion] of the remainder of the township without any reservation except the capital messuage, its garden, the mill which stands in front of its gate and the stewpond [fish-pond] and granary near the courtyard, which are to remain with Peter and his heirs."

The court document describes the manorial estate awarded to William and Peter with serious attempts at precision, in the absence of accurate measuring tools or reliable mapping methods.[8] William's portion amounted to 365 acres, in 61 parcels of land. He had six tenants, 13 villeins, mostly holders of 30 acres, and six householders, all probably in the village itself. On these properties there were two shepherds, a herdsman and a bailiff, who had a croft and a meadow. It is interesting to look ahead 130 years - to 1360 - to see how William's former estate had evolved. By then there were 110 acres of arable demesne land, eight acres of meadow and common pasture for 400 sheep, four working cattle and 12 oxen. Rents from free tenants were worth 29 shillings a year and 60 acres of land from bonded men were worth 38 shillings annually.

Peter Delamere's portion of the estate was made up of scattered pieces of arable land on the slope of the Plain, with grazing for sheep plus richer pasture to the north of the village. About half a century later (1272), at the time of death of his son Robert Delamere, the family had a variety of land parcels, including one for 40 oxen, another for 400 ewes, plus three water mills worth together 54 shillings and four pence annually. The overall income from the property was worth rather more than £15 annually. In 1292 this manor was owned by Robert's son, Peter, and it had 374 "poor acres upon the hill, and seven acres of meadow" (a little more than William's share), plus 88 acres on "sandy land" and 20 acres of much more valuable land in "deep land". There was pasture for 300 sheep, 16 oxen and six plough-horses. Rents from freemen were only 15 shillings, but from villeins the rents were an extraordinarily high £21 2s. 3d. By 1308 the Delamere manor had eight free tenants who paid a total of £6 11 shillings plus two pounds of pepper worth two shillings, annually. There were also five other holders of 30 acres, seven holders of 15 acres, nine bondsmen and ten cottagers.

The listing give clues to the sites of the manorial dwellings inhabited by these two lords. Peter Delamere's manor-house, the large courtyarded house, with a garden, a stew pond and granary with the mill "which stands in front of its gate," must have been near running-water to power the mill. All evidence suggests that the running-water was the stream which runs today through the Muddle. Later manorial records refer to a grove of trees in front of the house which became known as the Grove as early as 1327 [see John atte Grove, page 19]. So the Delamere manor-house - Market Lavington's first - was most likely to have been on the hill above the grove and close to the site of what was once Grove Farm house. Archaeological excavations, in 1995, on the hill above the original Grove Farm showed not only Saxon post-holes but also medieval material at the north-eastern end of the area. One grave was discovered but has not been dated. The other and somewhat later manor-house built by the Rochelles was the aisled hall[9] dating from the late 13th century which today survives, much altered, as the Old House. So in this early Lavington the manor-houses of two less than comradely lords probably flanked St Mary's Church and churchyard on the knoll above the village.

The only largely unaltered structure from this period which has survived is the Parish Church. The Delamere and Rochelle manors were probably built of wood and no traces of the Delamere structure exist in

---

[8] Among those parcels were eleven and a half acres of arable land "in the east of Groscrofte, a croft called Upper Horsgras." Other parcels, varying in size from a quarter of an acre to 55 acres, were mentioned as "Hamme at the end of the wood called Perrock, the western moiety of the marsh called Skymeresmore, land abutting on the road in Hokesburge," arable land "in Lokforlonge abutting on the bishop's land," tracts of 17 acres and 30 acres of arable land at "Ramadunesutende" and "Ramaduneshorthende" [clearly Saxon names], six acres of arable land "which lie next the land of William son of Maurice on the north," a quarter of an acre of land "next that of Master Robert in the east of Holedene," three acres "next that of Geoffrey, son of Simon, on the south," two acres of arable land "below the king's cross next the parson's land." The names of the meadows are splendid, though they scarcely roll off the tongue - Chapmannaweye, Westbrakedelonde, Ruwedunehille, Smallelonde, Chershsetlonde, Hulmede Brademede (one meadow), Newemilne, Madmanammore, Swynlegh, Skynerere, Burchlinkle, Raderygg, Ruwedunecumbe, and Berefurlonga. There is also one familiar name - Spyneshull - the Spin Hill of today.

[9] In earlier times a hall referred usually to a larger dwelling, often with a spacious central room.

any recognisable form. It is fortuitous that the wooden framework - notably the roof and some internal timbers - of the Old House remains and this is possibly because at an early date the wood walls were reinforced with rubble. About other dwellings in the Lavington of seven centuries ago we know very little, though it was a town of some size. One other description of a dwelling exists in the will of a landed proprietor, Patrick of Chaworth,[10] dating from the early 13th century. This will speaks of Chaworth's holdings "in the ville of Stepillavinton" as being "a certain long house in the place of a Hall, and one room in one head, another room in another head, cowhouse, of the court [sic] and two small barns, sheepfold on the hills, all said houses old and in a bad state." This "certain long house" was undoubtedly larger than the humbler houses which must have run west to east directly south of the church (the future Church Street), along the track which continued east (the present High Street) to Easterton and down Parsonage Lane into White Street.

ROCHELLE THE CRUSADER

William Rochelle was dead by 1234 but his son, Richard, prospered. A document in 1242 refers to his holding lands in three counties and in 1254 the King granted him a charter for a market at Lavington. His market in Lavington gave the village not one but two names - Market Lavington and Stupel Lavington - the stupel or steeple being the post driven into the ground marking the site of a market. The market did well. Documents of the time noted that the Rochelle market in Lavington in the mid-13th Century was "to the serious detriment of the market in Devizes." The Lavington market had rivals, however. When Henry III granted the Abbess of Romsey a weekly market at Church (later Steeple) Ashton in 1266 on the same day as the Lavington market, business suffered. Two years later Richard Rochelle complained to the crown that the value to him of his market had fallen by £40 - a very large sum at the time. When confronted, the Abbess of Romsey replied flatly that her abbey had no market at Ashton and no-one appeared prepared to argue with her. The Steeple Ashton market lasted nearly another two hundred years, until a disastrous fire ruined the village's economy.[11]

Richard Rochelle's horizons extended far beyond Market Lavington - further, indeed, than any other Lavington resident of the Middle Ages. He had legal training and was the King's Bailiff in Ireland, for which service he was granted lands there. In 1255 he was deputy to the Chief Justice of the province under instruction to survey land to the value of £500 in the safer portion of the territory on behalf of Prince Edward, later Edward I. A man of property, he owned manors in Ockendon and Crustwick in Essex and in Beckenham in Kent, and in 1253 he was granted special licence to hunt foxes, hares and cats in the Essex forests. He was also a man of parts - acting as a judge at Rochester, Kent, as castle custodian in Bristol, and as a tax assessor in London, and in 1261 as a businessman earning a £100 fee for equipping the Tower of London. More than once he intervened to secure the King's pardon for others.

Richard Rochelle must have built his aisled hall, the Lavington manor-house, between about 1240 (he was a minor when his father died in 1234) and before he sold it in 1268. The date 1240 is a little early, according to authorities on roof construction who have examined the roof-timbers of the Old House, but they agree that a slightly later date is likely. This date does raise the question as to where the Rochelles - and, for that matter, the Delameres - lived earlier in the century and during at least part of the preceding one. The Delameres may have built only once on their hill and the Rochelles may have used materials from an older house for the new one. In any case, Rochelle was a busy man and he could not have spent much time in the house in later years. His association with the village continued, however,[12] through the marriage of his daughter Margery to Andrew le Blunt, whose family held property in Gore. His sale, to Emmeline, Countess of Ulster and widow of Stephen Longespee, the second son of William Longespee, Earl of Salisbury, was probably in preparation for his departure on a Crusade with the future king.

Rochelle was among a small band of knights who joined Prince Edward at Dover, on 11 August 1270, on the largely abortive crusade to Tunis. Later, Rochelle was among the handful of knights, a thousand foot-soldiers and a few bowmen who travelled on to the Holy Land. Edward and his men raised the siege of Acre and carried the cross to Nazareth, which he captured from the Saracens. The Prince signed a ten year truce with the Moslems and sailed to Sicily where

[10] Chaworth was a man of substance and may have been of knightly status. His will refers to six virgates - 180 acres - of land leased out to villeins for a total of ten shillings annually. He also had seven half virgates - 105 acres - rented out at three shillings and four pence yearly. In addition the tenant was required to supply "three hens and one cock worth threepence halfpenny," annually. Among the tenants were Robert de Lavinton, Christiana la Custere, Roger Greneway and William Beaufiz, the last paying sixpence yearly plus one pound of cummin seed.

[11] In 1586 there were 16 market towns listed under Crown grants and one of these was Market Lavington. Swindon was not added to the list until 1626.

[12] It continues today in the name Rochelle Court, a modern building in the Market Place.

**An early photograph of the Spring, looking towards the village.
A baker's delivery van is on the left.**

he learned of the death of his father, Henry III. Later, the new King and his knights travelled on to Rome and jousted in France. The little band did not return to England until 2 August 1274. Coronations could wait the king's pleasure in those days.

EARLY JUSTICE

Litigation was part of the fabric of life in the Middle Ages and, as we have seen, the Lavington knights squabbled frequently, if harmlessly. But sometime before the Easter of 1249 the Delameres' confrontation with their neighbours took a more serious turn and the crime - murder - offers an opportunity to look at the system of justice practised in Wiltshire in these very early post Anglo-Saxon years. While justice in this instance was in the King's court, ancient ways still held. There were still so-called "kindred groups," who were outside the law, who smuggled cattle and refused to produce the guilty, if detected. There were the ancient "ordeals" aimed at proving the guilt or innocence of witches and others, and above the highest and the lowest were the clergy with their threats of damnation for those who dared to cross them.

Involved in the Delamere murder was Simon of Lavington and three members of the family, identified then as Thomas, William and Robert de Mara, or Delamere. This group accused six men of neighbouring villages of murdering one of the Delamere's kinsmen, Hugh. Of these Delameres, Robert was in direct line to succeed his father Peter as one of the two lords of Market Lavington manor. Accused were John le Mouner, Robert of Potterne, Geoffrey le Bole, William Pandulf, a chaplain, Ralph, nephew of the Dean of Urchfont and Adam le Lechur (the leecher, hence probably an early version of the general practitioner). The Delameres made the accusations directly to the County authorities, thereby ensuring a full judicial hearing before the Wiltshire "Eyre" or travelling court.

That hearing was at Wilton in Easter 1249, on 18 April to be exact, and the requirements of the law made it a very public one. An Eyre demanded that the county sheriff should summon four free men and a reeve, or churchwarden to the hearings, plus 12 burgesses - or municipal officers - from each borough, and for the Eyre at Wilton in 1249 some 600 men served as jurors, though not all were present at any one time. Many of the burgesses chose not to attend Eyre hearings unless they had a special interest in the proceedings, but there were witnesses to the case for the plaintiff and the defence. First there were the accusers, then the law required that four neighbours of the known person injured or killed should attend, plus, in the case of murder, the finders of the corpse. For the defence there was the accused and, if he had been freed on bail, those who had given sureties that he would attend.[13] The occasion was, as one can imagine, something of a Roman circus. Outside the court-room there were impromptu feasts and carousals, Mummers plays and a general air of high day and holiday.

There was nothing frivolous about the Eyre court proceedings, however. A Royal judge had great authority and it is a pity that there is no eye-witness reporting of the hearings. In fact, on the Delamere murder case there is only a dozen lines in the Wiltshire Crown Pleas of 1249 which summarise cryptically, as it does in most other cases, not only the accusations against the accused, but the course of the investigation and the sentences passed on them. This tells us that the defendants "do not come so let them be taken and their pledges for prosecution are in mercy." The time scale of this is misleading.

The six had not appeared to answer the charge, but by the time the Eyre court was in session three of the six were in custody. There are no details of evidence, or even where the crime was supposedly committed, but what we do have is the sentence and it appears that when it was handed down three of the accused were "outlawed."[14] One, Adam le Lechur, had been resident in Urchfont and in his absence his goods, to the value of 33 shillings, were seized for the Crown.

---

[13] The judicial reforms of Henry II created the "grand assizes" and the Eyre. Henry shrewdly saw that his new jury system should be built on the ancient one where villagers had given judgement - and meted out punishment. The criminal Eyre was the most cumbersome of the courts the King set up to make Royal justice more available. His civil courts were his so-called "grand assize," allowing four knights of the shire to chose, in the presence of a judge, 12 other knights to reach a verdict. Henry's achievement lay in allowing the commoner a hearing in a Royal court, with the judgement of a sworn jury of his peers, instead of trial by battle. As Keith Feiling says in his *History of England* the jury system survived in England primarily because it represented the public opinion of a neighbourhood and because it got a strong start in the assizes before it could be turned, under Canon-law influence, from an inquest into an inquisition.

There is a sobering footnote to the footnote: the reforms involved free men only. There was no new law to protect three quarters of the population - the villeins - who were still at the mercy of their lords.

[14] This was the process of putting a person out of the protection of the law and was a punishment for refusing to appear when called in court. From the earliest time it was the punishment of those who could not pay the blood-money to the relatives of those who he had murdered. He was too a "frendlesman" (the Saxon word) because he forfeited his friends and if any of them gave him assistance they became liable to the same punishment. It was not abolished in civil proceedings until 1879.

Robert of Potterne and Geoffrey le Bole were also outlawed, but whereas le Bole had no chattels to be seized, Robert's amounted to £8 18 shillings and two pence halfpenny - a considerable sum. The case against William Pandulf and Ralph, the Dean's nephew, took another course. The Court Roll says that "because they are clerks [they] deny to answer 'to the murder indictment' so let them be delivered to the Bishop's official who seeks them as clerks." This curious decision indicates that the two were not just clerks able to read and write - an early definition of a clerk - but clerks in the sense of being lay church officers and, under the law, they were indeed immune from the civil court. Their trial would come before their Bishop - and hence before God.[15] The Court Rolls report does say, in an apparent further reference to the two clerks and their subterfuge: "Let the facts be inquired into by the county." Nevertheless, say the Rolls, seemingly illogically: "The jurors say they are not guilty - so they are acquitted." What it may have meant is that the jurors could not find them guilty because they were under the Bishop's authority. They were lucky. The three who sought outlawry were beyond the reach of the court, but one of the six who, presumably stood his ground, John le Mouner, was hanged - and speedily.

Also soon hanged in connection with another murder was a Walter atte Grene, accused by a prisoner turned King's evidence of murdering a man at Biss. Grene took the man's horse laden with apples and sold it and then went on to Market Lavington where he met friends and together they burgled a house in the village and took goods valued at 26 shillings.

The court records for the next century - the 14th - show crimes ranging from the trivial to the most serious. Market Lavington had several. In 1303 Nicholas de Taunton was arrested for slaying Robert le Gerisshe in Market Lavington. He pleaded not guilty - as did almost every prisoner accused of serious crimes in these early centuries - and was acquitted by a jury. More we do not know, but it is worth noting as an indicator of the careless spelling of the time that soon afterwards a Nicholas le Borebrut was accused of slaying Robert le Serussh, again in Market Lavington.

Gerisshe and Serussh must surely have been one and the same.

Trivial but nevertheless recorded was the 1306 indictment before the Wilton court of John "nephew of the vicar" of Market Lavington for stealing fish from Robert Delamere's "stew-pond" - or fish pond - valued at 12 pence. He had broken into Delamere's "close" to do so. The penalty was not mentioned but it would almost certainly have been a fine, though the offence could have earned John up to three years in gaol.

HARD TIMES

By 1276 both Richard Rochelle, Emmeline, to whom he had sold the manor, and her elder daughter Ela were dead.[16] Ela and her sister, Emily, had inherited the manor jointly from their mother and Emily's son and heir, Alan, died in 1314. In his will he granted his share in the manor proper to a kinsman for life and to William Forestal forever in return for an annual rent payable to Alan and his heirs. The following year, 1315, was a grim one. Torrential rains brought agicultural devastation to the whole of Europe that summer and contemporary histories speak of families eating their horses and dogs in futile attempts to stave off starvation. Wheat was inedible unless dried out in ovens and even then it sold for six times its normal price - to those who could afford it. In this time of stress and tumbling land values, Emily de Lacey, who had her half share of the Market Lavington manor, granted three acres of manorial land and the living of St Mary's Church to the Archdeacon of Wells, Robert de Wanborough, who became rector. Emily required Robert to say prayers twice daily for her, for his brother, for himself, for Richard Delamere and for others.[17] Robert appointed vicars and in 1329 he installed his brother John as rector, and later another brother, Thomas, also became rector.

The hard times continued and throughout the 1320's the number of oxen was halved in south-eastern Wiltshire, and arable land - the land which fed the people - fell in volume sharply on many big estates. The value of manors like Market Lavington also fell and when Emily died in 1331 the share in the manor

---

[15] The trial before the Bishop's "spiritual" court was called "purgation," or purging. If the accused failed to purge himself he could be condemned to lifelong imprisonment in the Bishop's prison, which, by all accounts, was by no means as severe a place as, say, Old Sarum gaol. Bishop's prisons were also notoriously easy from which to escape and there is an implication that Bishops were often glad to be rid of long-term prisoners because of their cost of upkeep.

[16] The Rochelles' sale of the manor ends their recorded association with Market Lavington, but in 1330 at a camp at Moyalby, a knight who was almost certainly linked to the Lavington Rochelles or Rokeleys, Sir Richard de la Rokel, was made a Knight of the Bath and in 1513 Thomas Rokeley was knighted at Lille. Knighthoods conferred abroad suggest that the descendants of the old crusader, Richard Rochelle, continued the tradition.

[17] It is worth noting the names of the three witnesses to this sale - William of Lavynton, Robert of Hungerforde, William Forestal and John of Escote - men whose identity was sufficiently established by their home towns or villages.

proper, as opposed to the church living, which she granted to William Forestal was of less value than the one her sister had given him. Nevertheless, Forstal had both of the original de Lacey shares, leaving the remaining half of the original manor in the possession of Robert Delamere's son, Peter, who was a 15-year-old at the time of his father's death in 1308. He received a grant of free warren in his demesne lands in Market Lavington ten years later and it was he, who, in the 1340's, founded a chantry chapel in St Mary's Church.[18]

An event of significance for Market Lavington came in 1337 when the vicar of St Mary's granted the church's living, plus an acre of arable land "east of the high road leading to Salisbury," to William de Montague, Earl of Salisbury. Undoubtedly the most renowned name to be associated with Market Lavington in its long history, William was Marshal of England, crusader and "the mirror of all martial men," as a contemporary source dubbed him. It was he who wrested the dreadful Richard Mortimer, Earl of March, at the behest of the 18-year-old King Edward III and thereafter William was the King's most cherished companion in peace and war. Though his family seat was at Montacute, Somerset, his place was by Edward, who gave him an eagle for his crest, an eagle which the King alone also bore. In Wiltshire, William had manors at Amesbury Earls, Trowbridge and Winterbourne Earls, but he sought out the acre of land and the living of St Mary's, Market Lavington, and later we shall suggest why.

The former Rochelle portion of the Market Lavington manor remained for a few decades with the Forestals and the Delamere portion descended for another two centuries through a series of marriages until the time of the Reformation. By this time the Delamere portion of the manor was known as Lavington Baynton and later Lavington Dauntsey, both the Baynton and Dauntsey families having an interest in the property. We know little about the Forestals, the new owners of the Rochelle portion, by now known as Lavington Rector, other than that they were no strangers to the courts. The name appears first in connection with a non-payment of rent in Lavington, plus homage and service owed by William de Forestal and his heirs. The next dispute, in the Assizes of 1331, was about ownership of the manor involving four members of the Forestal family and there were further court-cases in 1344.

252 TAX-PAYERS

Though harvests were down through natural causes another factor was the growth of the wool industry. As the demand for cloth grew, landowners grazed sheep on land which had provided crops.

At this time, four years before the onset of bubonic plague or the Black Death in England, Market Lavington had 252 poll-tax payers - about as many as Chippenham - which suggests that the population was approaching a thousand. Though Salisbury has about 12 times as many, Market Lavington was above average in size and about 16th in size in the county. Devizes, with 302 tax-payers, was the 13th largest town.

---

[18] The Delameres' chief legacy was the chancery chapel, but may also have left their name, slightly corrupted, in family names known in Market Lavington as late as the 19th century. A Dinah Dalimear had her daughter, Elizabeth, christened in 1795 at St Mary's; another daughter, Mary, christened in 1797; a son, James, christened in 1801; and another daughter, Jemmima, christened in 1803. Elizabeth's daughter, Marianne, was christened at St Mary's in 1819. Further afield there was an Alice Dellimere married in Devizes in 1620, and a large family of Delimears living at Seend in the 18th century.

TURBULENT CENTURIES

THE BLACK DEATH

One reason why few 14th century timbered houses have survived in Market Lavington and elsewhere is because the Black Death brought panic-burning of infected dwellings. The plague spread in the west country from the ports of Bristol and Weymouth in 1348. On 24 October the Bishop of Winchester, William of Edington, of whom we shall hear much more in another context, issued a stern and biblically colourful warning to his diocese via the clergy. "Much weeping and crying has sounded throughout the various countries of the globe," he began, and then continued: "Cities, towns, castles and villages, adorned with noble and handsome buildings and wont up to the present to rejoice in an illustrious people, in their wisdom and counsel, in their strength and in the beauty of their matrons and virgins; wherein too every joy abounded and whither multitudes of people flocked from afar for relief; all these have already been stripped of their population by the calamity of the said pestilence, more cruel than any two-edged sword. Into these places (of plague) now none dare enter but fly far from them as from the dens of wild beasts. Every joy has ceased in them, pleasant sounds are hushed and every note of gladness is banished. They have become abodes of horror and a very wilderness; fruitful country places without the tillers, thus carried off, are deserts and abandoned to barrenness."[19]

Even William's colourful style did not do justice to the horrors which had befallen Europe, however, striking at a society which, though it had experienced war, had known its enemy. Here the enemy was beyond comprehension, and attributing it to sin and God's displeasure, or for that matter to the work of the Devil, did nothing to halt its depredations. Probably no later than the bleak midwinter of December 1348 or January 1349 the plague was provoking panic in Winchester, Salisbury and Wells. The well-to-do were taking to the roads north with their retinues and valuables, and with them they took the disease[20] and villagers in Market Lavington, near cross-roads north and south, east and west, were soon struck down.

To whom could the villagers turn? There was the vicar but the vicar was only mortal and, as a constant visitor of the ill and dying, he would have been among the first to become infected and a replacement would probably not have been forthcoming. There was the village elder like the reeve, or churchwarden, usually a more approachable figure, whose concerns were the day to day management of village affairs, but if he survived, he would have been a desperate man. The temporal lords of the manor were an alternative, but we must assume that the joint owners, the Delameres and the Rochelles, were either well barricaded in their houses or had taken to the roads like so many others. Finally, because desperation and ignorance provoke desperate recourses, the villagers would have turned to those who today we would describe as the lunatic fringe - the soothsayers, the purveyors of wonder drugs, the witches and the simple - those who might have "an answer" when all else appeared to have failed. Suddenly the "dark ages" of their forefathers seemed nearer and villagers would have resorted to a frantic search for a panacea or resigned themselves to the ugly inevitable.

In all villages like Market Lavington one of the first steps the inhabitants took was to isolate themselves from neighbouring communities, because the villagers could say with some justice that those who brought the evil tidings from beyond the Plain also brought the disease. So men armed and ready to use their weapons would be sent to bar the roads.

Then there was the problem of where to bury the bodies and who was to bury them in that terrible first winter of the plague? Initially - that is for a few weeks - the village sexton and helpers would have permitted the use of St Mary's graveyard during the short daylight hours, but very soon the villagers, like villagers and townsfolk across England, were turning against the burial of corpses so close to their homes. Pits were dug in remote fields, and bodies collected over days and weeks were buried as one. Within a few months, by the summer of 1349 at the latest, law and order must have been near collapse.

We will never know how many died in Market

---

[19] This warning to clergy showed Edington accepting the medieval attitude to sin and its punishment: ".......it is much to be feared that man's sensuality which, propagated by the tendency of the old sin of Adam, from youth inclines to all evil, has now fallen into deeper malice and justly provoked the Divine wrath by a multitude of sins to this chastisement."

[20] The Bishop of Bath and Wells issued a proclamation to the Diocese in January 1349 saying that "No priests can be found who are willing, whether out of zeal and devotion or in exchange for a stipend, to take on pastoral care ...... nor to visit the sick and administer to them the Sacraments of the Church [perhaps for fear of infection and contagion]." He suggested that those who were dying without the comfort of clergy should make confessions to each other - "even to a woman." His implicit attack on his own pastoral assistants was probably unfair. Many would have died already. We know that nearly 48 per cent of the clergy of Bath and Wells did not survive.

Lavington in 1349-1350 but the plague cannot have spared it any more than neighbouring villages and towns. Nationwide about a third of the population succumbed and it appears to have been higher in larger population centres like Salisbury, Winchester, Bath and Wells, where nearly half died. Based on the poll tax returns suggesting a population of about a thousand, this means that in Market Lavington more than 300 people died directly from the disease.

The survivors in villages like Market Lavington inherited a different economic landscape. Where hundreds had tilled the fields of summer and autumn, in the first summer after the plague there were only scores still able to work, and when strangers from other villagers arrived to work - even though it was likely they had run from bondage to their lord - they were welcomed as extra pairs of hands.

THE EARLY CHURCH

There is no mention of the church of St Mary in Doomsday, but there are indications that the present 14th-15th century edifice was built on the foundations of a Norman church which, in turn, may have been built on Saxon foundations. Relics of the Norman structure survive in a string course of carved stones found during the 1862 reconstruction, which are now built high up on the wall on the inside of the porch. There is also now a bowl in the vestry forming a piscina which is also Norman and the narrowness of the south aisle may indicate the layout of that portion of the Norman original.

There are signs too of an earlier floor than the present one. The earlier one was laid to a slope following the natural level of the ground, falling from north to south. The present north door, now unused, was about two feet six inches higher than the south door and with the later levelling, the sill of the north door is now that height above the floor. The crude finishing of the bases of the older pillars in the north aisle also show where the floor was lowered and the foundations of the pillars exposed.

The church's exterior is built of ashlar and sarsen stone and has a chancel with north and south vestries, and a south organ chamber, an aisled and clerestoried nave with a south porch and a west tower. Inside the church, the east and west windows of the north aisle are late 13th century which suggests that the nave had achieved its present proportions by that time.

The chancel may be as old as 1300 and the north vestry and porch are of various dates in the 14th century. The south arcade and two bays, a door, and west and east windows of the north aisle, and the lower part of the walls of the south aisle, are about the same date.

In the mid-15th century the wall of the south aisle was raised and a two-light window was built into the added part. The three-light windows appear to have been inserted into the south wall in the 17th century.

The beautifully-proportioned tower is 15th century. It has buttresses in all sides and the west window and door are treated as one feature, with bold projecting jamb and arch mouldings carried to the ground. Interestingly, oyster-shells are freely used in the joints of this construction.

The staircase to the rood loft starts from the site of this chapel and is a 15th century addition, as are the door arch and the little trefoil windows. The stairs are well preserved and the passage to the loft is only 18 inches wide.

In the nave the windows are remarkable. There are three of the original single-cusped lights on the north and two on the south. On the north side there is a very late, probably 16th century, three-light window near the east end, probably inserted to throw more light on the rood-loft, and a two-light window of the same date in the centre of the south side. Both of these windows have heavy wood inside lintels.

The south porch has a good inner doorway with cusped arch, probably of the 16th century and there is a good corbel over the outer doorway and part of an ancient cross above. There is a rude sundial cut in the south-west buttress of the porch, not indicating the hours of the day but it might once have shown the canonical hours.

The sacristy dates from the late 14th century and the corbels of the old roof remain. The squint in the chancel wall points in the direction of the high altar and was probably intended for the use of the priests.

The first known Vicar of St Mary's, named John Erdescote, was appointed in 1299 for a brief stint of three years. None served for long during those early years, however. In the 31 years before 1330 there were eight vicars. It is interesting to note that Robert de Wamburgh was vicar for a year from 1315 and then became an intermittent patron of the living until 1329. The de Wamburghs were influential men in the ecclesiastical world of Wiltshire then and later.

USLY, AMITH, PROSPER, DOVE

St Mary's Parish Registers date from 1622 and for the first few years they were written partly in Latin. There were usually three churchwardens, each holding office for a year. Several of the early ones were unable to write and signed the entries with their "mark."

Among the families appearing in the registers before 1670 are Axford, Birt, Bishopp, Edwards, Giddings, Gye, Hurrle, James, Lye, Oram, Planake, Potter, Shergold, Spire and Still. There are Christian names associated with these which are still in use, but others are rarely if ever heard: Gulie, True, Shadrach, Siller, Usly (all male) and Amith, Prosper, Albina, Janevereth, Kalcheren, Dove, Genenra, Barbery and Friseweed, all female.

There are baptismal entries in the register with some opportunistic spelling:
"I.T. Edeth and alian dafters [daughters?] of water

St Mary's Church and the graveyard, circa 1905.

The Muddle circa 1910. Houses toward the Church Street end were formerly the parish workhouse.
The Vicarage was later hidden from this point by new buildings on the right in Church Street.

The path from Broadwell to Church Street, circa 1920, before houses were built in the Mead.
On the left is a thatched mud wall.

The Spring, in 1916. On the right are Spring Cottages (Nos.20 and 22).

venell July 8 1633."

"Ann day [daughter?] of Willi fiveash Sept. 13 1663"
"William son of Mary Harris (married to Wm.Kelly a soaldier as she pretends) Feb. 14 1692."
"Elizabeth, daughter of a poor travelling woman going to Dover named Hackman, April 23rd. 1699."
"Shadrack, Mesech and Abednego, sons of William Briam Feb. 22 1713." (There is an entry noting the burial of the triplets eight days later).

THE CHANTRY CHAPEL

What must have been the most interesting monuments in St Mary's are, however, missing. These were associated with the chantry chapel of Saints Katherine and Margaret, which has lent lustre to the history of an otherwise modest village church. The Reformation erased virtually all signs of the chantry chapel but its site is not in serious dispute. It occupied the east end of the north aisle and was most probably separated by screen work from the rest of the building. Beneath the east window, of three unconnected trefoil lights, there are distinct traces of an altar, and in the north face of the eastern pier of the nave arcade, close to the east wall, is the accompanying piscina, also trefoil-headed. All wanton destruction is, of course, a tragedy, but the Reformation's destruction of this historic chapel within the church of the Blessed Virgin was a double tragedy.

Peter Delamere obtained a royal license to build the chapel and he financed its future maintenance as a religious monument by carving from his manorial estate in Market Lavington a holding of several houses and 13 parcels of land amounting to 27 acres with pasture for 50 sheep. Income from this investment paid the living of the chaplain in charge. In return the chaplain was to celebrate mass daily in the church of the Blessed Virgin ".....for the good estate of the said Peter while living, and for his soul when he shall be withdrawn from this light, for the souls of his ancestors and heirs and the souls of all the faithful departed....."

It cannot have been a coincidence that the consecration of the Delamere's chantry in 1343, was at the time of a visit to the church by William Montague, some six years after he had purchased the church living and became its patron. William was a devotee of the Delamere chantry's patron saint, St Katherine, who had a curious attraction for the English nobility in the Middle Ages and Renaissance.[21] What was to become the great monastic church at Edington was re-dedicated in 1354 to St Katherine by William of Edington, Bishop of Winchester and Chancellor of England, and Peter Delamere was already associated with an even older dedication of a St Katherine chapel at Wanborough.[22]

So what did men like William Montague and at a lesser level, Peter Delamere, find so beguiling about these chantry chapels in these out of the way villages and towns? Chantries had, in fact, become fashionable. The old urge to found monasteries was passing and the emphasis was on the importance of saying masses for the dead and it appears those who founded them regarded them as talismans, albeit religious ones. William had a special devotion to the cult of St Katherine, but he almost certainly had associations with other chantries and, like his contemporaries, he saw them as a form of insurance. Peter was 50 and William was 42 at the time and no doubt both were looking with a clear if not untroubled eye at the eternal life which they and their contemporaries believed awaited them. The chantries were to buy not only eternal life but eternal life in heaven through the purchase of eternal ritual on earth. The custom of "presenting" oneself at a chantry involved the appointing of a priest who would supervise the ritual and was, in effect, a rehearsal for presentation before the Almighty, and often, but not invariably, involved gifts.

William died the year after his visit; having survived[23] terrible battles in Scotland and France he was

---

[21] In 1929 a bronze seal of the 14th century was dug up in a garden at Spin Hill. It is a little more than an inch long and shows the Virgin and Child and a kneeling figure above. Below is the figure of St Katherine. The inscription on each side reads "Mater Dei" and "Miserere me."

[22] This had been founded by Emmilene Longspee who, as already mentioned, inherited Richard Rochelle's portion of the Market Lavington manor on his death in 1276. After her daughter Emily's death in 1331 the rent from the Market Lavington manor, worth 14 marks a year, went into the coffers of the warden of the earlier chapel of St Katherine there. This Wanborough chantry was known to Peter Delamere. Commemorated in it were a contemporaneous branch of his family, headed by William and Agnes Delamere. No trace of it remains, again thanks to the Reformation. It is believed to have stood at Court Clonear, Foxbridge, more recently called "Cold Court."

[23] Before his departure for a "crusade" (presumably to France) in 1335 William went with all his family and train for last prayers at Bisham Abbey, which he had founded. His daughter, who was in a convent at Marlow, joined him there "with her nuns," as the story goes. Among those in attendance on her father was a squire who had been in love with her and he seized the opportunity for elopement. They escaped in a boat, but were captured, presumably by William's men, at Marlow. William sent her back to her convent and the squire was shut up in a tower, from which he tried to escape by means of a "rope made of his clothes and sheets." The rope broke and he was "dreadfully injured." He was taken back to Bisham Abbey, where "he afterwards became a monk."

Photograph taken from the Market Place, looking towards Northbrook. The houses on the right were known as the Terrace and were demolished in the 1950's. The site is now part of Rochelle Court.

Mr James, the baker, delivering bread from his cart, at the foot of Lavington Hill.

killed accidentally on the jousting field.[24] Peter had five more years to live before his wishes were carried out. The date of his death, 1348, suggests he may have been an early victim of the Black Death but he was 55 - a considerable age for the time.[25] Peter Delamere's son, Robert, was 32 in 1348 when his father died, and one of his first acts as patron to the Lavington chapel was to appoint a priest to it and the following year William's widow was a visitor. The Montague's direct association with the Delamere chantry was brief, however. It ended in February 1354 with a charter issued by William's son, the second Earl William of Salisbury, granting the Market Lavington church living and the acre of land which went with it to William of Edington, Bishop of Winchester. It is worth noting that among witnesses to this transfer were four knights.

WILLIAM OF EDINGTON
We look now at a more powerful and more direct influence on St Mary's, Lavington, by one of the truly remarkable men of his time, William of Edington. Born to parents of no prominence in the humble little village of Edington as the old century waned, he took the name of his birthplace, as so many other villagers did at the time. He may or may not have been a member of the ancient family of Cheney of Brooke Hall, Westbury, but in a career of remarkable diversity, William became Treasurer of the Exchequer, Chancellor of England and in 1346 bishop of Winchester, the first prelate to hold the Order of the Garter. Finally he was Archbishop-elect of Canterbury a few months before his death.[26]

It was, however, the then unassuming Edington church and properties in the neighbourhood which he had known since his birth for which he reserved some of his energies in his later years. In 1344, when he became Winchester's bishop, Edington was under the control of the Benedictine Abbess of Romsey and was neglected, and through his extensive secular and ecclesiastical contacts he obtained the right in 1351 to form a new religious foundation and set up a chantry of three chaplains, ostensibly to pray for the souls of himself, his father, his mother, his brother, the Royal family and the bishops of Salisbury and Winchester. And like Peter Delamere, he chose that the chantry chapel should be dedicated to St. Katherine, as well as the Blessed Virgin and All Saints.

In fact, William, a great builder and a man of enormous drive, had a broader vision for his new foundation. By mid-1352 he was seeking annexation of a chapel at Maiden Bradley, largely it seems, so he could afford to double the number of his chaplains to six. And when the first stone of the new church was laid, he decided to convert his College into a monastery. The undertaking was becoming more expensive and demanding and in his search for income he must have been encouraged by the readiness with which Salisbury's second Earl transferred the Market Lavington living to him (see end of previous chapter). In December 1354 he used this impending transfer as an argument to increase the number of his chaplains at Edington by an additional four - to 13.

The Edington Cartulary dates the physical transfer of Market Lavington's living to Edington as 13 August 1355 and, thanks to the literacy of the clergy we have not only the date but we know who attended this transfer. Assembled at Market Lavington on that high summer day were Bishop William himself, John St. Neots, the Bishop's brother John of Edington, Thomas of Stuplelavington esquire, Edward of Chirdestok and Philip of Upton. It was probably Edward Chirdestok who took notes. It is fascinating to picture one of the powerful men of the kingdom arriving at St Mary's by horse - he rode everywhere - accompanied by some of his 132 servants.[27] The sight

---

[24] This was not uncommon. Several European kings and princes died jousting in the 13th and 14th centuries and two hundred years later Henry VIII, at the age of 32, suffered a near fatal blow to the head from a lance. Historians have suggested that the blow changed his personality - for the worse.

[25] In the early centuries death usually came later to the nobility because of their more nutritious diet, but even so several of England's early rulers died before they were 50. Henry IV was 46; Henry V was 37; Henry VI, 40; Henry VII, 46; Edward I, 48; Edward IV, 41; and Edward VI, died of tuberculosis at 16.

[26] "A good friend... to the Commons whom he protected from royal extortions, and assuredly a good friend to the King, Edington has left only a faint impress on the pages of history; something of the anonymity of the model civil servant still clings to him. Yet it is likely that the successful financing of the war in the years of victory owed more to him than to any other single man." (May McKisack : *The Fourteenth Century*)

[27] He always carried with him a travelling set of chapel fittings, or cappella, carried on two horses so that he could conduct a service wherever he found himself. He also travelled with a kitchen staff, a poultry man, a brewer, a baker, a pantry-man, a buttery and a squillerie or scullery. Each of these had to be sufficiently adaptable to set up in any residence the Bishop wished to visit. The portable chapel followed William in a cart, then followed two more carts carrying baggage and each cart was in the charge of a page and a boy. Then came the Bishop's clerical staff on horseback. As Bishop of Winchester he owned some sixty manors in seven different counties - Somerset, Wiltshire, Hampshire, Berkshire, Buckinghamshire, Oxfordshire and Surrey.

of the procession must have been the great event of many of the villagers' lives.

The Edington Cartulary document on the transfer of Market Lavington provides more than just the date of the transaction, however. It records that Philip of Upton had resigned as rector and that Walter Scarlet, warden of the new Edington chantry, "entered the Parish church of Stupellavynton..... and took corporal possession of it, received the canonical obedience of the perpetual vicar, sang mass in the chancel, and took possession of the rectory house."

Where was this rectory house? An agreement dated 18 January 1360 says that the rector of Edington, and Richard, the new vicar of Market Lavington, had agreed that "the vicars shall have the house and close formerly assigned to the vicar, one virgate and tithe-free rights of common [grazing] for four oxen, two beasts and a hundred sheep" pastured with those of the rector." In addition, this document records, the vicars shall benefit from "all great and small tithes" and "mortuary fees" from the entire parish, including the chapel of Gore (excepting mortuary fees "arising from the deaths of the lords there)" plus tithes on "foals, doves, calves, geese, piglets, mills, flax, hemp, milk, hens, bees, garden curtilages, wood-coppices, the profits of merchants, alehouse-keepers and other workers in the Parish." Here was taxation indeed! In return, "the vicars shall pay all outgoings from the said church and chapel and they shall provide bread, wine, and lights, and provide and maintain as necessary books, ornaments and vestments for the church and chapel." The Market Lavington rectory was established on firm ground thanks to its influential spiritual brother in Edington.

THE BONHOMMES

These Edington priests were new to Wiltshire. The charter granting Winchester's Bishop the right to the new monastic order, signed on 29 March 1358, spoke of his "long desire that the church and the secular society united with it should be elevated into a religious house wherein would be settled the brethren of the Order of St Augustine, commonly called Boni Homines by whom as by vigilant husbandmen, a garden of healthful plants may be watered and, by the help of the Lord, produce rich and ripe fruits, flourishing in the House of God." The church and the monastic order were created "to the honour of the Blessed Virgin, St Katherine and All the Saints." The Bonhommes had been recommended to William of Edington by the son of Edward III, Edward the Black Prince, who had seen their work in France, there being only one other foundation in England, at Ashridge, in the county of Buckinghamshire. [28]

The new, imposing priory church, which still stands, was completed in 1361, by which time William was busy with further plans for expansion and he negotiated for the purchase of lands in manorial estates in various counties. To do this he had to have cash and cash he had, thanks to his previous employment, as Treasurer of England for 12 years and as Chancellor for six. As a buyer of lands he had to take whatever was on the market and he had to buy piecemeal, but he bought relentlessly.[29]

He had already been given the living and associated properties of the Market Lavington Church and now he set about acquiring the Forestal share of the Market Lavington manor, with the chapel of Gore dependent on it. He negotiated with Robert Forestal, the son of the man who had acquired the property from the Rochelles. The sale was completed in 1368, two years after William's death[30] and the church held the manor with payments of 20 shillings a year to Devizes Castle, five shillings to the preceptory of the Knights Hospitallers at Ansty and £9 6s. 8d. a year to Emmilene Longspee's chantry chapel of St Katherine at Wanborough.

The Edington Cartulary makes it clear that the Bonhommes had installed a vicar of their choosing in St Mary's, Market Lavington, in the 1360's, but it is unclear to what extent they were able to extend their holdings in the village. What they did own they almost

---

[28] The qualifications for becoming a brother of the house were that candidates should be of good character, competently learned, under no kind of bondage of debt or service, unmarried, and suffering from no incurable malady. When asked what their object was in joining, candidates were to prostrate themselves on the ground and reply: "The mercy of God and truth." The Warden who William placed in charge was provided with a separate house but he and the chaplains under him were to eat together. Guests were allowed for meals - dinner costing them three pence and other meals two pence. All chaplains were to avoid taverns and could not enter houses other than their own without the Warden's permission. They were permitted to speak to women only if they were their mothers or sisters and, at least in the early years of the Foundation, they were asked to restrict any conversation. The impression is, however, that their order was comparatively relaxed for its time.

[29] William moved remarkably swiftly to extend his monastic demensne. By 1361 he had acquired a number of properties in Edington itself, the lands in Market Lavington, others in Coleshill, Berkshire, property in North Bradley, in Tinhead, the manors of Alvescot and Albury, Oxfordshire, of Tormarton in Gloucestershire, and Westwell and Erlestoke, plus the church livings or parts of the livings of the parishes of Kimpton in Hampshire, Buckland in Berkshire, and Bratton, Melbourne, and Stoke in Wiltshire, plus rents in Kingston Deverill and a life interest in the manors of Bratton and Eastrop.

High Street, circa 1910. The far end of the Kings Arms was a separate cottage
later incorporated into the pub to enlarge the bar.

White Street, circa 1910.
Trees are growing at what is now the entrance to the car park area. The heap of stones is for road repairs.

A view towards the Church from the foot of Lavington Hill in the 1950's.
The cottages on the right have since been demolished. The barn on the left is still roofed with thatch.

Looking towards the Plain from outside Hillside Cottage at White Street.
The cottages on the left were demolished in the 1950's.
The sheep were being moved from pasture on the Plain to West Park Farm.

certainly leased out and the manor at Market Lavington became known as the manor of Lavington Rector, a reminder to all that the Superior of the order of Bonhommes, the Rector, was the owner at least of the living. It was in later centuries, when the monastery had long since been dissolved, that the manorial farm of Lavington Rector was known as Rector's Farm, with the former manor house, the aisled hall - one day to become the Old House - known as Rector's Farmhouse.

The Bonhommes in Wiltshire appear to have prospered, though without William the pace of their expansion slowed. They added parts of the manor of Dilton in 1381 and the living of Keevil in 1393 and they survived inspections of monastic title by the Canterbury Archbishopric. In 1382 a new Rector was elected from the 18 candidates. One nominated was Thomas Lavynton, but he had to wait until nearly 1400 to become Rector. Ownership by the new, illustriously-supported order of brethren must have given prestige to Lavington Church and maybe this is the reason that members of great families like the Beauchamps, Tocote and St Amands appointed their priests through the years to the little chantry in the Church of St Mary.

The Bonhommes were not only prosperous but too worldly for some tastes in later years and they provoked some tart comments. In 1662 Thomas Fuller, in his *Church History*, said that "these Bonhommes tho' begging Fryars and eremites.....tho' pretending to have nothing..... would not cast their caps (I should say their cowls) at rich revenues if bestowed upon them, but contentedly (not to say cheerfully) embrace the same." And two centuries later the Reverend Arthur Fane in his brilliant description of the Edington Church said: "Probably from that time to the dissolution the Monastery of Edington contained the usual amount of knowledge and ignorance - of true devotion to God, and hypocritical pretence - the same amount of zeal and apathy, of virtue and vice, which at this day is to be discovered in any community of men." Quite.

Throughout the nearly 200 year link of the Edington monks with St Mary's, the Delameres and those who followed them remained faithful to Peter's chantry. Robert Delamere returned to the chapel two

years before his death in 1381 and his widow Matilda continued the tradition by appointing a priest to the chapel in 1403, the year before her death. She stipulated in her will that she should be buried in the church precincts. Her son, Peter, died eight years before her and as he had a daughter, Willelma, and no sons, the manor passed to Willelma. She died in 1410 and was buried in Bromham Church, "near her lord." She had, however, already granted the Delamere portion of the manor to Walter Beauchamp, Sheriff of Wiltshire from 1402 to 1404,[31] and he too became patron of the chantry.

Beauchamp continued the Delamere association and in his will of 1429 he asked to be buried in the Delamere chantry. His wife, Elizabeth, also kept her ties by appointing a priest to the chapel in 1434. In 1436 she made it clear when she associated herself with the church at Whaddon that her ties with the chantry continued by signing her name Elizabeth Beauchamp of Lavington Forum (another name for the village) and in her will of 1446 she also asked to be buried in the Market Lavington chantry near the tomb of her husband.

The association of the Beauchamps with the Delamere chantry continued at an exalted level in 1450 with the appointment of a priest to the chantry by William Beauchamp, the eldest son and heir of Walter and Elizabeth.[32] At the time he was in Parliament as Lord St Amand and Chamberlain of North Wales, the title by right of his having married Elizabeth, heiress to the Barony of St Amand. He also asked to be buried in the chantry on his death (in 1456). Elizabeth remarried - to Sir Roger Tocotes, a man of many parts. Twice Sheriff of Wiltshire, he was accused of treason against Richard III, but was cleared with Richard's overthrow and then given the office of Constable of Devizes Castle and the Knight of the Body and Comptroller of the Household of Henry VII. But great man though he was, he and his wife were jointly patrons of the Lavington chantry, though his tomb is in Our Lady's Chapel at Bromham. The curious fixation with the chapel in the simple little church in Lavington continued into the next century. Richard Beauchamp, the son of William

---

[30] William's will of 1366 is a remarkable document in which he disposed of legacies which came to more than £2,000 in cash. Every church with which he had been connected closely and every member of his Episcopal household or staff was remembered. Here is an extract: "And to Robert, my body servant, I give 10 pounds, and to John Romsey, my barber, I give five pounds, and to the boy in the bakery, five pounds, and to Thomas, the carter the elder, ten pounds, and Philip and Thomas, who work in the brewhouse, five pounds each, and to William, the boy who leads the first, cart five pounds, and to John the boy who leads the second cart, five pounds...... My soul I leave to Almighty God, my creator; and my body to be buried in my cathedral church at Winchester in the nave at the point where the monks make a halt on Sundays and Feast Days, as they go past in procession, or elsewhere in that church, if the prior and my executors should think that more fitting." He remembered his monks and he remembered, in the end, humility. He achieved his wish to be buried in his beloved Winchester Cathedral. He is not in the nave, but in an aisle. There he sleeps in his chantry chapel, with a finely-executed marble figure. Only his foot-cushion, probably a couchant lion, appears to have been damaged by the Commonwealth's vandals. The face is that of a churchman of the time - not aescetic or severe, but with a relaxed, secure expression. He had, after all, got what he wanted.

Beauchamp and Elizabeth Lady St Amand, continued patronage of the chantry in 1490, again in 1504 and yet again in 1506, as did his wife Anne. The Barony of St Amand died out in 1508 and this branch of what had brought together the Delameres and Beauchamps became merged in the Wiltshire family of Baynton.

The Baynton family had held the manor of Fallardeston or Falston in Bishopstone, south Wiltshire, for many generations and few families of any period can have sought fame and found both fortune and misfortune so persistently. Sir Henry Baynton was a Knight of St. John of Jerusalem and Knight Marshall to Henry II (1154-89). His son, Henry, was slain in Brittany, in royal service, in 1201 and a later Sir Henry Baynton was beheaded at Berwick for taking the part of the Earl of Northumberland against Henry IV (1399-1413). By 1450 the Bayntons were again in favour but in 1471 Sir Robert Baynton plotted the overthrow of Edward IV (1461-1483), was imprisoned and barely escaped with his life. His son, John, lived quietly at Bromham, dying there in 1516, but his son, Edward, soon knighted, became a confidant and adviser not only to Henry VIII but, as Vice-chamberlain, to three of his Queens - a high-risk job for any man. Edward prospered, however, and no doubt because of his prosperity and position in court he succeeded in marrying Isabella, the granddaughter of Thomas Duke of Norfolk.

Isabella happened also to be the half-sister and lady in waiting to that most ingenuous and foolish of Henry's Queens, Catherine Howard (beheaded before she was 20). Sir Edward and Isabella Baynton were the first to learn of Catherine's confession to the Primate Cranmer of her adultery before marriage to the King, and the Bayntons were to survive her indictment, in effect, for promiscuity (a "crime" with which the King had had much first-hand experience). By the Reformation the Bayntons had their reward with liberal gifts of monastic lands in Wiltshire and elsewhere. Sir Edward built a new mansion in Bromham and acquired an old manor house at Corsham and in 1522 he leased West Lavington manor, or Lavington Baynton as it had come to be called, to William Dauntsey, a merchant. Sir Edward was also patron of Market Lavington chantry chapel and hence in control of the estate associated with it. He appointed a priest to the chantry in 1537 and because the lands of Edington Priory were sequestered by the Crown as part of Henry VIII's vengeance on all things Roman, his was the last appointment to the Delamere chantry. What had begun as one suppliant's faith in eternity had supported 15 chaplains over its

nearly 200 year history in a modest village church.

The chantry property which fell into the Bayntons' possession consisting of two houses, an orchard, two fisheries and pasture worth annually £3. 15s. 4d. in rents from numerous cottages. After Sir Edward's death in 1545 it reverted again to the Crown briefly and then in 1551 Lady Isabella Baynton obtained a lease, remarried, and moved into the chantry house of Edington Priory buildings, living there or in the neighbourhood until her death in 1573. It is most likely that she visited St Mary's Church more than once over those two decades. The elaborate "gentrification" of Lavington Rector's farmhouse (the Old House) dates from the mid-16th century, so it is likely that one of the two houses which she owned in Market Lavington was made more liveable for her occasional occupation. After Isabella's death her son, Henry Baynton, sold the largely destroyed Priory and land to Sir John Dauntsey, in 1590, and, undoubtedly, the further improvements at the Lavington Rector Farm, including panelling and additional fireplaces, came with the Dauntsey ownership.

THE REFORMATION

The chaos of the Reformation was particularly felt in Lavington. The high altar went the way of the Delamere chapel and as late as 1553 the rubble of the altar and other ornamentation of "the Papists" was still piled in the chancel. The old service books in Latin were destroyed and replaced with a Bible in English, but the church had no Psalters for a number of years. There were also regular inquisitions about whether parishioners were still using rosary beads. The church living was granted in 1556 to Christ Church, Oxford, and the chapter there is still patron of the living.

By 1671 Market Lavington was going its own way on the controversial subject of holy days. Those days falling at harvest time were ignored in many county villages but in Market Lavington they were ignored also if they fell on market day. In 1676 there were 476 churchgoers in the parish and in 1783 there were about 40 communicants. On Census Sunday 1851 there were 300 at the morning service, and 250 in the evening. In 1864 there were 80 communicants. In 1875 the vestry passed a resolution that in future St Mary's vicars should wear the black gown in the pulpit because it was "more in accordance with the principles of the Reformation and generally more acceptable to the parishioners than the surplice."

Few, if any, of the early rectors lived in the parish. Among later vicars was Nathaniel White, who

---

[31] There is an unexplained reference to a "transgression" against the King in the official recognition of this transfer. The Patent Roll of Henry IV says that Willelma granted the manor to Walter and Elizabeth Beauchamp and then adds that "We [i.e. the King] of our special grace and for one hundred shillings paid into our hanaper [a department of the Chancery] have pardoned the transgression of the said Walter and Elizabeth......"

[32] William's younger brother, Richard Beauchamp, was Bishop of Salisbury and first Chancellor of the Garter.

The High Street in 1905. The Workmen's Hall is on the right and the house to the
right of it was part of a private school run by Miss Chinnock.

Formerly the Market Lavington Vicarage until the late 1940's,
now part of the Northbrook Nursing Home in the High Street.

Russell Mill and the Manor kitchen garden.
Russell Mill, formerly in the parish of Market Lavington, was at one time the home of the Saunders family.

The Post Office in 1905 was on the site of the chemist's shop,
and the house on the right of it was part of a private school run by Miss Chinnock.

was ejected from the living in 1660, and Arthur Brett (died 1677), the reputedly mad poet. One rector whose name is unrecorded was sufficiently put out by his argumentative parishioners as to resort to the courts to control them. The Devizes Quarter Sessions of 1647 heard him petition that he had been "several times molested by some of his intemperate parishioners and lately was publicly opposed in the Church in point of doctrine by Thomas Barley and immediately in the churchyard by John Whatley to the great disturbance of him, of his Parish and the diserpation [dissemination?] of the gospel." The assize judges appear to have been unimpressed by the petition and a footnote is appended to it saying only: "It fell out to be but a discourse in the Church. No action taken."

The only other recorded example of parishioner restiveness comes from the church records of a much later date - 1871. The vestry passed a resolution that the churchwardens give formal notice to John Williams that "because of unseemly conduct...... he be not permitted to occupy the pew hitherto appropriated to him," and "in case of need" he should be summoned before the magistrates.

TAXES

Taxes in Britain are at least as old as the Romans and in earlier centuries fell into two chief groups - income tax and tithes. Broadly speaking, income taxes financed the adventures and excesses of the aristocracy and the tithes paid for the shepherding of the religious flock. The taxation rolls of past centuries tells us not only something about the cost of running the country and the court but where the money was and who had it. So we find that in Market Lavington in 1545 there were six members of the middle class considered as being tax worthy. There were probably several members of the aristocracy in the neighbourhood, but they were assessed separately, if at all. Most of them arranged to be tax commissioners. The 1545 tax was called "a benevolence" and was described by that most unloved and unlovely of men, Henry VIII, as "a loving contribution" required from all his well-to-do subjects to help him fight wars with the Scots and the French. The six, with their assessed contributions in brackets, were: John Heyre, gentleman (40s.), John Heyre junior (6s. 8d.), Richard Hull (20s.), John Seynsburye (20s.), John Coke (10s.), and John Hyscocke (5s.).

Thirty-one years later, when Henry's daughter,

Elizabeth I, needed a special levy for military commitments in Ireland and to further the Protestant cause in France and the Netherlands, she sought two shillings and eight pence in the pound for a first instalment and 16 pence in the pound for the second. Paying £5 on this occasion were John Hampton and John Westall, paying £3 were Richard Peers, John Hoskins, John Foster, Amys Peers, John Seinysbury (the Sainsbury family again), John Brothers, John Tailor, Joan Dowce, Leonarde Dowce, Christian Synsbury (another Sainsbury)[33] and William Bishop, and paying a pound, Richard Hoskins. The second tax brought 13s. 4d. from Hampton, 8s. 4d. from Westall, 5s. each from the rest, except for Hoskins who paid 22s. 8d. None of these were truly large middle-class landowners. John Dauntsey, in West Lavington, who had large holdings, paid £20.

EARLY INDUSTRY

The major industry of Market Lavington for at least six hundred years was textile manufacture based on wool. The Saxons ran large flocks of sheep and as early as the *Doomsday Book* Tilshead was an important collecting centre for the wool industry which had spread across the downs and uplands and by the 13th century there were sheep-flocks of more than 2,000. In seven Wiltshire villages in the late 13th century the peasants owned four times as many sheep as their Monastic landlords, and often the villeins were able to buy their freedom and land as well.

The seat of the wool industry was in the north-western half of the county. Here conditions were ideal for textile manufacture as the fuller's earth, almost indispensable for the thickening of broadcloth, was available along and under the edge of the downs, from Westbury and Edington to the Lavingtons and, further north, toward Rowde and Calne. The Avon and its tributaries supplied the clear water necessary for scouring the cloths when they had been "fulled" and also provided motive power for driving the mills. Some of the wool was grown locally, but larger and finer supplies came to north Wiltshire from the Cotswolds, the Welsh marches and the grazing country of the Midlands.

Weaving was an ancient craft and weavers' guilds date from the reign of Henry I. The industry began to expand rapidly in the early 14th century and by 1350 a prosperous cloth trade had grown up centred

---

[33] The sheer size of the Sainsbury family in Wiltshire is staggering - and confusing. An Anne Sainsbury married in Market Lavington in December 1784, an Anne Sainsbury married in Bromham in 1785, an Anne Sainsbury married in West Lavington in 1786, an Anne Sainsbury married in Trowbridge in 1788, an Anne Sainsbury married in Little Cheverell in 1789, an Anne Sainsbury married in Steeple Ashton in 1793, and an Anne Sainsbury married in Erlestoke in 1796. There were also Ann Sainsburys and Anni Sainsburys married in the same period as well as Sainsburys with most of the other 25 letters of the alphabet for initials being born, being christened, marrying and dying. The only other name which rivals Sainsbury in its frequency in Market Lavington's neighbourhood is that of Giddings, with its many variations in spelling, and the Giddings' seem to have arrived first (there was a Vicar called Gyddinges at Market Lavington in the 14th century).

Greenhouses under construction for Mr Crisp, at Fiddington Hill, during the late 1920's.
They were manufactured in Somerset, erected by Fred Burgess of Easterton,
and glazed by the King family of Market Lavington.

An R.A.S.C. steam traction engine collecting water for the military forces on the Plain
during the First World War.

on Salisbury, Winchester and Bristol. At this time Wiltshire was only the tenth most populous county in England, but only Norfolk, Kent and Gloucester collected more taxes. In 1377 Salisbury was the sixth largest provincial town in England and by the next century the city saw the growth of a cottage industry outside its walls which was beyond the guilds' jurisdiction.

Wiltshire specialised in the making of undyed broadcloth, chiefly for central European markets. As early as 1346 Guild regulations in Bristol stipulated that the looms of anyone weaving inferior cloth should be destroyed. The regulations also prohibited craftsmen from working at night so that all weaving would be done in the sight of anyone. The industry met the demands of the expanding European markets by moving outside the restrictions of the guilds and by adopting the so-called domestic system. This brought cloth production to the villages and smaller towns and specialisation even within the family unit was a feature of the 15th and 16th centuries. By 1550 it was estimated that fourteen people were required to produce a piece of cloth. In 1552 new clothing statutes prescribed that each broadcloth should be 26 to 28 yards long and should weigh at least 44 pounds. Before it reached the consumer, the raw material had to pass through the hands of carders, spinners, weavers, fullers, dyers and shearmen, to name but a few of those involved. Obviously there had to be some link between these crafts people and the market, and here the clothier played a part.

There was a true cottage industry in weaving all over Wiltshire as Daniel Defoe noted when he took a journey through England between 1724 and 1726. He spoke of "innumerable villages, hamlets and scattered houses, in which generally speaking, the spinning work of all this manufacture is performed by the poor people; the master clothiers who generally live in the greater towns, sending out the wool weekly to their houses, by their servants and horses, and, at the same time, bringing back yarn that they have spun and finished, which then is fitted for the loom." Market Lavington was one of the villages involved in this cottage industry and the villagers looked to Devizes clothiers for their outlet. Readily available wool was an asset and Defoe estimates that Dorset, Wiltshire and Hampshire had access to two to three million fleeces a year. The Hungerford family made Heytesbury, in the Wylye valley, south-west of Market Lavington, their main breeding centre in the 14th century and the Hungerfords kept flocks of more than a thousand sheep on several of their manors. West Wiltshire wool reached London on pack-horses making the long journey from Devizes via Marlborough

The clothier was usually himself a cloth worker but as his function involved little technical knowledge, the position came to be held by outsiders who often combined it with other pursuits like sheep-rearing, tanning or general farming. The clothiers became the moving force not only in their trade but in the west of England propertied hierarchy. Typical of one clothier was Thomas Horton (died 1549), whose family had prospered in the textile trade under the early Tudors. He lived in Iford Manor, near Bradford on Avon, and had business interests in Devizes and properties in Bradford, Trowbridge, Keevil, Chippenham and Box. He also grazed 350 sheep on Lavington downs and spent much of his life travelling, whether managing his widely-scattered properties or attending the London markets.

It is interesting that the booming domestic textile industry did not produce centralisation of production as was already happening in the 16th century in coal and iron mining. One wealthy clothier, John Winchcombe, with Stumpe of Malmesbury, assembled cloth workers under one roof in a very primitive factory, but he encountered hostile legislation in the Weavers Act of 1555 which limited the number of looms in one house. The Act was meant primarily to discourage the growth of rural industry and the expense of the towns. Additionally, technical progress in weaving and spinning was slow until well into the 16th century. The textile workers in Lavington and other villages like it were specialists and usually did not do agricultural work. The exception was when there were fluctuations in the demand for cloth - usually brought about by diplomatic quarrels between England and the Continental countries which took the English cloth. Then there was unemployment - lasting, sometimes, for years - and the cloth workers returned to the land.

The cloth industry left its mark on the domestic architecture of west Wiltshire. Cloth merchants built St Mary's, Devizes, and the splendid church at Steeple Ashton owes its architecture to cloth. And clothiers built great manor houses like Great Chalfield, Westwood Manor and South Wraxall. In Market Lavington, where the industry had been tied to the individual weaver, traces of the weavers' cottages must be sought in the High Street houses which have been much altered through the centuries.

Decades-long European wars brought a decline in the wool industry in Wiltshire by the mid-17th century, though with the loss of the European markets new ones opened at home. The boom of the earlier years never returned. By the first national census of 1801, Wiltshire had fallen to 24th in terms of population, and 16 other counties had more people. Part of the reason for this was the development of mechanisation and the growth of Yorkshire milling. Wiltshire had 50 mills in 1838 but only 17 in 1871.[34]

---

[34] A few handloom weavers survived, but so did prejudices. An historian tells of a Yorkshire weaver who abandoned his livelihood because he would not work with women in the mills. He chopped up his loom and grew cabbages.

Another industry was brick-making which employed men in the village from early times. In later years it became centred on an area of pasture north of the village which has a heavy clay content. It was here that the Market Lavington Brick Works began operating in the early 19th century. The so-called Gault Clay made the excellent red bricks which built many of the village houses. The brick-works manager's former residence still stands beside the works, which are now offices.

Maltsters followed the barley and the barley grew in profusion on the Plain. In the 18th century there were 27 malthouses in the village - most of them home brewing - and some survived until early in the 20th century. Within the past hundred years malthouses were at work in Parsonage Lane, at the site of the Scout Hall, Beech House office and Gye's workshop in White Street, and at other less clearly defined sites. A family living in the White House ran a wagon service to London breweries.

A craft said to be unique to Wiltshire and brought to its highest level by a Market Lavington artisan, Tom Smith, is dew-pond making. Dew-ponds were in demand when farmers moved onto the chalkland downs and lacked a piped water-supply. The precise details of dew-pond construction were kept secret, but involved digging a large hollow, packing it with clay, then slaked lime, then straw and finally hard-packed rubble and stone. The finished product was a pond which depended on rainfall at first but which heavy dew (hence the name) would top up. Tom Smith is gone, but his ponds, mostly overgrown with grass because they are no longer in use, dot the uplands. One, made between the Wars, is on the track leading from Eastcott to the "Greenroad" above the village.

THE PLAGUE'S RETURN

The plague was not confined to the Middle Ages, even in west Wiltshire. In 1604 the Salisbury authorities issued an order against wandering rogues and vagabonds who allegedly were spreading disease. Complaints were made of people who refused to stay in their homes though they had been in contact with the plague and those who were found to have done so were imprisoned for a month. Market Lavington is not mentioned as being among settlements infected, but Devizes and Marlborough suffered and in October the plague in Westbury so isolated the town that the authorities arranged for Market Lavington and Warminster to supply middlemen from Westbury with corn.

The plague was again in Devizes in 1607, and in 1610 Bradford had the disease for 20 weeks. In 1625 Salisbury had a day and night watch to prevent the arrival of visitors who might be carriers and two years later 369 citizens of the city died and many others fled into the countryside. In 1637 a later Sir Edward Baynton engaged a London physician to try to stem an

outbreak in Calne and he stayed two months. A Devizes outbreak of 1644 prompted the authorities to impose a weekly tax on all citizens within a five-mile radius, but all thoughts of taxes to save lives were put aside in the search for money to wage war.

THE VILLAGE AND CIVIL WAR

Upraising from the bed of toil,
Springs every tenant of the soil:
The gentry their retainers arm,
And propagate the wild alarm.
The drinker starts, that sound to hear,
And half suspects his flowing cheer,
Then quaffs the rest to quench his fear;
Oh! who would scorn good Wiltshire beer.
From out each hamlet, field, and dale,
The lusty peasants troop apace,
Arm'd with the deadly scythe and flail,
Or brandishing a rustic mace.
Still as they pass, their ranks increase,
And shouts of vengeance rend the air:
"We'll crush the traitor to our peace,
Or hunt him to his very lair."

So said a Bristol poet in would-be heroic vein as he described the Wiltshire Clubmen, as they were known, a 3,000 strong local association, which grew from the chaos and devastation of the civil war between the Royalist Catholic supporters of King Charles I, the Cavaliers, and the Protestant Parliamentarians or Roundheads. Market Lavington's chief role in the war was as part of the campaign by the Clubmen to end the hostilities. The Clubmen were groups of farmers and artisans who decided early in the conflict that they would not take sides but would urge an early peace. Inevitably, as Royalist and Roundhead sacked their homes and destroyed their crops, they did take sides and there were more Royalist Clubmen than Roundheads. Some of this support for the Monarchy had also been attributed to the countryman's traditional conservatism, particularly in the west of England. As one of their contemporary critics said, they wanted "the old vanities and superstitions of their forefathers, the old necromantic order of prelacy, and the wondrous old heathen customs of Sunday-pipings and dancings, with the meritorious maypoles, garlands, galliards and jolly Whitsun-Ales."

There were geographical variations in the Clubmen's support for the King, however. In general the so-called cheese country of north Somerset and Wiltshire was Royalist and the chalk downlanders, with their long hours at the plough, who had less time for the fancies of court, were for the Parliamentary party. There was, however, much opportunism in the Clubmen's support of either cause. If the war went well for the King, as when Prince Rupert captured Bristol, he had more rural support, and so too did the

Commerce in the High Street during the early 1920's. From the left, a boot and shoe repair shop,
a photographer, the Co-op Stores, and a corner restaurant. Mr and Mrs A. Burgess are standing in front
of their home from which they ran a photography business, which was later carried on by their two sons.
The Burgess family took many of the photographs reproduced in this book.

Church Street circa 1910. The Hopkins family ran the Ironmongery Store,
and accommodation for touring cyclists was provided at what is now the Doctors' Surgery.

Roundheads when they forced Rupert's garrison to surrender the city.

Described as the war without an enemy by one of its greatest generals, the Civil War can be divided into three phases, beginning with Royalist victories in the summer of 1643, including their capture of Devizes. The second phase opened with the Royalists losing the initiative to the Earl of Essex's army in June 1644. The third and ugliest phase of the conflict, lasting another year, saw Somerset, Wiltshire and Dorset devastated by local murderous, destructive skirmishing and raiding by both sides. This final phase, ending in the triumph of the Parliamentarians, came when the so-called New Model Army took the field in June 1645 with Oliver Cromwell at its head.

Market Lavington villagers were impelled on pain of imprisonment or death to fight for whoever recruited them and whenever and wherever they were ordered to, but generally speaking they were for the Parliamentary party based in London. The professionals at the head of largely untrained armies on both sides scoured the villages of Wiltshire for men. Both armies had run short of recruits very quickly and the villages were a ready source of supply. So it was that in 1644 the King's generals needed 667 from the county on short notice and they issued a proclamation pressing men into service. Market Lavington escaped that call to arms, but village constables received instructions to round up 21 recruits from both Potterne and Cannings. Specifically needed were any able-bodied, fit, single workmen (or "mechanics" as they were called) and tradesmen (but not mariners or preferably not husband-men) and they should be "conveniently apparelled." Untrained country lads that they were, they did not survive long after their arrival at the front around Devizes, which was then in the King's possession. Later proclamations issued by the opposing Parliamentary forces at a more desperate time called on all able-bodied men from the surrounding villages to present themselves within four days at Devizes with spades, shovels and pick-axes to demolish the King's fortifications there.

Market Lavington first heard the cannons of war loud and clear on 11 July 1643 but this was the culmination of long and bitter months of pillage in the countryside around Devizes and as far as Malmesbury, Marlborough and Pewsey. At this time Devizes had seen a succession of Royalist commanders, including the notorious Sir Thomas Lunsford's and Lord Digby's murderous troopers - "the boys for havoc" as they were known. Lunsford's dragoons usually slaughtered whoever opposed them in the villages but in March a raiding party which had stolen oxen, horses and cloth encountered a force of Clubmen and Clubwomen about a hundred strong and armed with one musket, forks and halberds at the hamlet of Ogbourne. The dragoons fled and the news spread that the villages in north Wiltshire were firmly against the King - or against his minions, at least.

The Parliament's best general, Sir William Waller, had left Hampshire for the north in early March and he decided to attack the northern border towns in Royalists' hands. He took Malmesbury and then lost it when he left it insufficiently defended when he went on to Gloucester.

The cannons which Market Lavington heard on 11 July were forged by the Commonwealth, captured by the Royalists and fired by them at the Commonwealth troops on Roundway Hill, east of Devizes. The Roundway Hill battle has long been regarded as the high point of the Royalists' campaigns and it would be nice to report that it was a set-piece masterpiece in the Napoleonic mould. It was far from it.

The manoeuvring around Roundway began on 10 July, when the Royalists concentrated their entire force of 3,000 troops and 500 horsemen on rising ground east of Devizes, awaiting the arrival of the Commonwealth's men. Waller's force had, however, already arrived and it took some time for the Royalists to realise that the force of nearly 5,000 dragoons and raw foot-soldiers were not a Royalist, but an enemy army. When they did, they retreated into Devizes and Waller installed a seven-gun battery on the hill they had left. The next day the bombardment of Devizes began and on 12 July Waller's cavalry charged into the town - to be met with streets blocked by anything moveable.

The Royalists called for a parley - which they prolonged for six hours - long enough, in fact, for Royalist reinforcements - nearly 3,000 lifeguards under the King's nephew Prince Maurice, Lord Crawford and Lord Wilmot - to reach the town's outskirts. Waller's men, now tired and wet from constant rain - retreated to Roundway Hill.

At 4 p.m. on 13 July the Royalists, combined into one army, provoked Waller to charge three times and each time he was beaten back. Wilmot's reserve of 500 then counter-charged and Waller's forces broke and fled down Bagdon Hill. His pikemen stood firm, but soon were mown down by the cannons the Royalists had captured. Waller and most of his cavalry escaped to Bristol and the King's army triumphed.

The long-term result was the impoverishment of north Wiltshire by an administration - if that is not too grand a word - determined to make the country people pay the King's bills. Three of the "hundreds," the administrative divisions at that time, were fined £1,000 each for furnishing Waller's army with provisions and many families had to leave the land and live as beggars in the towns. Naturally this rapacity did nothing to earn the Royalists friends, particularly in villages like Market Lavington.

In the Market Lavington area the special enemies of the north-west Wiltshire Clubmen and their families were the dangerous and ruthless Royalist raiding parties which made sorties from Devizes during the long Royalist occupation of the town after the

An illustration of the Independent Chapel, built originally as a Friends Meeting House, taken from
A Topographical Account Of Market Lavington by the Rev. H. Atley, published in 1855.
The building with a small graveyard is opposite Stobbarts Road.

Interior of the Congregational Chapel (now Trinity Church) decorated for
Harvest Thanksgiving in the early 1900's.

Employees at the Brickworks in the early 1900's, when the works were owned by the Holloway family. The works were on the site of the factory at Broadway.

Early employees of T.H. White, with agricultural implements, at their premises adjoining the Market Place (now part of Rochelle Court). Mr Parsons, wearing the bowler hat, was the foreman. The young lad is a Burgess and seated is Mr Cooper.

victory of Roundway. These raiding Cavaliers took anything they could carry or rustle. Their activities are well-described in a contemporary letter to friends in London from an inhabitant of Bromham, where Cavalier soldiers were quartered at Sir Edward Baynton's magnificent manor-house. The King's soldiers "rove about our county, where our misery is such that we are forced to pay them moneys to eat up our provisions for we must allow every common soldier six pence by the day, bedsides diet, 12 pence per sergeant, 18 pence the lieutenants and captains," says the writer.

Market Lavington encountered the raiding Royalists several times and one such raid came on 11 May 1645, during the last phase of the war. The Royalists had detected a force of Roundheads marching north from Amesbury and the Cavaliers were sufficiently alarmed to abandon Baynton's manor at Bromham, having set fire to it and its contents. They raised the alarm in Devizes and a force of dragoons clashed with the Amesbury troops between Devizes and Lavington. The Roundheads retreated to Market Lavington and according to one Royalist source the Cavaliers pursued them and found seven or eight in a village tavern. The report adds sarcastically that these men "having preferred their bellies to their safety were brought with such triumph into Devizes that...... I doubt not but it will prove a great victory, for he [the King] hath few others of late."

A much more serious encounter came two months later, on 10 July when the Royalist commander in Devizes ordered his adjutant, Major Dowett, to raid Market Lavington for money and valuables to help pay for the King's cause. The Cavaliers decided to attack the most eminent house in the area at the time - that of the staunch Parliamentarian Sir John Danvers in what is now West Lavington. Danvers was on duty with his regiment, but he had left his factotum, named Merryweather, in charge. Merryweather locked himself in and went to the kitchen for a pan and pestle. He then ran to the upper floor of the house and in the words of a contemporary report, "commenced a most deafening clatter..... for the purpose of arousing his neighbours to a sense of his position and of their own danger." Downstairs the Royalist troopers hammered on the main door with their swords and soon the villages of both West Lavington and Market Lavington were alerted.

In Market Lavington villagers ran to the market square and rang the bells which hung there and as this had been a signal of the Clubmen along the foot of the Plain that an emergency was upon them, the whole area was soon in uproar. The Clubmen of Urchfont, Eastcott, Cheverell and Erlestoke took their weapons - largely scythes and pitchforks, and headed for the Lavington cross-roads.

Dowett and his band soon saw they were vastly outnumbered and retreated in the direction of Devizes, but the Clubmen, now a thousand strong, formed into a long, legion-like column and followed them to town. They encountered no resistance and, arriving in the Market Square, turned left and assembled in front of the Castle. Leaders stepped forward and called for Sir Charles Lloyd to present himself. He did not do so, probably because he was at Lacock, where he spent much of his time. Spokesmen for the Clubmen shouted that they would not be "plundered" and one speaker referred to the "better example" of the Commonwealth commander Sir Thomas Fairfax, who, the speaker said, had only days before executed one of his dragoons not eight miles from Devizes for having looted.

The Clubmen soon dispersed unharmed but the incident did have some affect on the Royalists' conduct of their campaign. For the first time they realised the danger of a large-scale uprising in the countryside and Lloyd made it clear to Dowett that he should be careful where he raided. Dowett went much further afield and, sadly on a raid only a few days after the Market Lavington incident - in Collingbourne Ducis, his men killed a farmer who refused to pay on demand.

It was an ineptly fought war but, as in all wars, thousands of professional soldiers and thousands more of raw recruits died or were disfigured and thousands more starved. This is shown most vividly by the veterans' and widows' petitions for pensions. These petitions spanned decades and were addressed to Justices of the Peace sitting in special sessions beginning in 1662 - some 17 years after the end of the Civil War. In Wiltshire 327 veterans or their families obtained pensions if they could prove they had served their long-since executed King.

Market Lavington had three such pensioners: John Hobbs the elder, from Easterton, a husbandman; William Tayler, and Phillip Dowse. Hobbs' story, related in his plea of 1661, is typical of so many. He said he was a trooper in "the late King's service" for almost two years under Captain Hugh Grove in the regiment of Colonel Sir George Vaughan as part of the brigade of Prince Maurice. In this service he lost two horses of his own worth £16 and "lost one of his fingers by a wound in his hand and received other hurts to the disabling of him to strive in the world for his maintenance as in former time he could." In addition, his petition says, he was plundered of his goods by the Parliamentary forces to the value of £10 and was imprisoned at Winchester by the Parliamentary forces for two months, "where it cost £20 [a bribe?] before he could get out." All this, he said, "amounts to his damage and hindrance to the sum of £100." The Justices awarded him 40 shillings a year, about average for pensions to veterans other than officers. It was, however, small compared with his erstwhile wage as a trooper - two shillings a day.

In Phillip Dowse's case, heard in 1666, the Court considered "the poor condition and sufferings of a soldier in the late Wars of his late Majesty" and thought fit to increase his pension from 30 to 40 shillings a year. Of William Tayler, the remaining Market Lavington parishioner to receive a pension, we know only that he received a pound, also in 1666. He was luckier than some, who received nothing, and luckier than others who found their pensions reduced for one reason or another.

Among the most inadvertently amusing petitions before the Justices was one from a publican in the neighbouring village of Potterne. Thomas White petitioned a year after the war about a visit to his tavern in 1643 by Sir William Waller. White said Waller had directed his officers to seize from him "for the Parliament service" as much beer, strong water and sack as came to the sum of 54 pounds or near thereabouts and carried the same to a place called Roundwayhill with promise to pay for same, since which time your petitioner has oftentimes demanded the same but cannot receive any satisfaction by reason of the backwardness of the Parishioners who do refuse to contribute towards the same." It appears not to have impressed White that his tavern's alcohol went to sustain Parliamentary troops on the eve of one of the most famous of Royalist victories. The Justices reserved their judgement on his lost casks, perhaps because they remembered that Waller's well-provisioned troops had lost the battle, thereby nearly losing the war.

THE PLAGUE AGAIN

The aftermath of war had not long left the west of England before the plague returned and this time the authorities took draconian measures to try to curb it. About the time of the great outbreak in London (1665) Trowbridge and Marlborough set up pest-houses, to which any sufferers were removed. Stray dogs and cats were killed on sight, but there was not even a mention of the real culprits, flea-carrying rats. In July 1666 the whole of Wiltshire was called on to pay £100 a week additional taxes for 20 weeks for the relief of the plague in Salisbury, where the mayor reported that 52 houses had been sealed, thereby incarcerating 196 citizens. Another 23 families were in the pest-houses and 1,855 citizens were on relief.

Only a few easily-identified graves remain of the victims. Many were burned, but an exception is the site known as Three Graves, between Market Lavington and Urchfont. Here lie the remains of John, Jacob and Humphrey Giddons, brothers who died in a plague outbreak in 1644. There is no trace of the minister of Urchfont Parish, Peter Glassbrook, his son and four grandchildren, who died that year and were buried by a maidservant, the only survivor in the Vicarage.

THE NEW MIDDLE CLASS

Detailed records are few for the Lavington manors - Lavington Dauntsey as well as Market Lavington - in the mid-17th century. There is, however, one document, the 1631 will of Sir John Dauntsey, which

surveys what it refers to as the Chantry manor in Market Lavington which he owned at the time of his death. The manor included three properties, 200 acres of land and 100 acres of pasture, and listed are the 19 tenants. Together they paid to the Dauntsey estate £217 13s. 4d., of which £60 was paid by one John ffilkes [sic] alone. Other names mentioned in the will are Thomas Purchase, Robert Coleman, Isaac Selfe, John Holloway, Edward fforth [sic], Moses Ruddle, John Mattock, Robert Sainsbury, Nicholas Norris, Richard Hopkins, William Gibbs, Bridgett James (widow), "the widdow Lye," William Wise, Richard Night, Oliver Crawley and Henry Jackson.

Dauntsey's will perpetuates the clear distinction between the manors of Lavington Baynton and Lavington Rector and appears also to make a distinction between properties in the Lavington Rector manor and in Market Lavington itself. The Lavington Rector portion refers to two properties, plus two cottages, 40 acres of land, ten of meadow and 12 of pasture. It seems likely that the Old House was one of the two properties. Dauntsey's heir was his grand-daughter, Elizabeth, wife of Sir John Danvers, who died in 1655. His estates passed to his daughters, Elizabeth, wife of Robert Villiers, who assumed the name Danvers; and Anne, wife of Sir Henry Lee. The manor of Lavington Rector seems to have passed to Anne (died 1659) because in 1662 it was held in trust for her two daughters, Eleanor and Anne. Eleanor married James, Lord Norreys, and Anne married Thomas Wharton, created Marquess of Wharton and Malmesbury in 1714.

By the latter half of the 17th century prosperous farmers and craftsmen without title or lineage were moving into the village, first as lessees and much later as outright owners. The chantry estate changed hands several times. Gabriel Still of Market Lavington, a farmer, acquired leases on it in 1661, by which time it included 17 houses, 90 acres of land and ten acres of meadow spread over the countryside as far as Seend. It does appear, however, that Rector's Farm (the Old House) was separated from Still's large estate because in 1671 John Slade, gent, held a lease of a portion of the original holding at an annual rent of £11 and his home was the old manor house, Rector's Farm. The property included three other small leaseholds, six farms, including one attached to an inn, and colourfully named fields like Home Close, Walnut Close, Goosemead, Lord's Wood, Bottom Meadow and Hamwood.

The leaseholds did not, of course, affect the outright ownership of these properties by the gentry. So in 1681 Anne and Thomas Wharton sold their share to Anne's sister, Eleanor, and her brother-in-law, James Norreys. Lord Norreys became the Earl of Abingdon the following year and it was from Abingdon that a prosperous village craftsman, John Samwell, became lessee of the Rector's Farm manor. The price Samwell paid for the lease is unspecified in his later will but much else indicating how the new middle class

The Elisha family and others outside their tailoring and sewing machine shop on the corner of Chapel Lane.

White Street, circa 1912. The Brewery Tap sign can be seen just right of the centre of the photo.

The Potter family aboard their horsedrawn 'bus outside their house next to the Green Dragon.
Mr Potter operated a 'bus and carrier service to Devizes until about 1916.

craftsman lived is detailed. His parents in the village were John and Beata Samwell, and he married in 1672, at the age of 26, "a spinster of Comb", the 20-year-old Sarah Slatter. He died in 1711 and his will names not only Rector's Farmhouse as his leasehold property but also the Allington parsonage, valued at £800, a substantial sum, which he left to his daughter Grace. He also had another leasehold property - the Market House in the market place, which he left to his sons John and Thomas. Grace (born 1692), the youngest of his children, also received the furniture of the Old House parlour chamber, while Thomas (1682-1751) received his grandfather's silver tankard. The children were left £10 each to buy mourning clothes. The inventory of the furnishings in the Old House valued them at £3,000 - a very large sum at that time. The furnishings, suggesting a comfortable way of life, included an organ, valued at £20, two tables and 16 leather chairs, a punch ladle, four table cloths and three dozen napkins, four dozen plates, and two gross (288) bottles, presumably forming a wine-cellar.

REBELLION

It was, however, the Earl of Abingdon who continued as owner of the Samwell leaseholds and being a prominent landowner did entail responsibilites - and risks - which his lessees did not encounter, unless, of course, they were recruited to fight for his cause. In 1685 one such cause had Abingdon joining the Berkshire militia to put down the attempt by the Duke of Monmouth to wrestle the crown from his uncle, James II. It is unclear whether he recruited locally before joining the Berkshire Regiment, but one record refers to a party of the King's army in the west marching from Lavington and halting, presumably as a rear-guard, at Devizes for two crucial weeks during the brief campaign.

Market Lavington's role in the rebellion remained peripheral, partly because Monmouth's rebellion was so short-lived that the King had no need to search far for volunteers. Monmouth was the late King Charles II's illegitimate son who had been in exile in France for six years. He landed at Lyme Regis, Dorset, on 11 June and died on the scaffold on 15 July.

Extracts from a cryptic diary written by a young foot-soldier in the Wells Militia captures the hectic manoeuvring of the two armies and we can only wonder at the strength of the men who could march through the day and half the night, but who were always ready to stand and fight when required:

"June 20 1685: in afternoon marched from Sarum (Salisbury) to Wilton, nine miles.
June 21 on Sunday in afternoon from Wilton to Lavington, 16 miles.
June 22 Lavington to Chippenham 14 miles.
June 27 Bath to Trowbridge seven miles, heard sounds of battle at Phillips Norton [now known as Norton St. Phillip].
July 7 Battle marched from Middlezoy to King's Sedgemore, hanged six rebels from sign-post of White Hart Inn, and afterwards marched 11 miles to Glastonbury.
July 8 Glastonbury to Wells to Phillips Norton 18 miles, arrived near midnight .
July 9 Phillips Norton to Devizes 18 miles.
July 10 Devizes to Sarum [via Lavington] 18 miles."

The battle to which the diary refers is the battle of Sedgemoor. The site is open country three miles south-east of Bridgwater. In the mists and watercourses of farmland unfamiliar to Monmouth's raw recruits the King's army cut them to pieces. Monmouth fled but the King's men captured him in Cranborne Chase.

DISSENTERS

The theme of dissent has been part of the Market Lavington historical framework for centuries. The House of Tudor was the first to seek unification of the kingdom through religious uniformity in the form of the established church and those who refused to become communicants in this church were called non-conformists. Under Elizabeth I the last of three Acts aimed at this uniformity compelled the use of a new *Protestant Prayer Book* and imposed fines of 12 pence a week on absentees from church service. By the 1630's the north-west of the county, including Market Lavington, inclined to Puritanism and nonconformity, while the so-called cheese country of the south was traditionalist and conformist.

The spread of Presbyterian adherence in Wiltshire churches is shown by a letter from the Wiltshire ministers and pastors sent to their brethren in London in 1647, after the triumph of the Parliamentarians and the establishment of the Commonwealth. This letter declares support for "the truth of Jesus against the errors, heresies and blasphemies of the times and the toleration of them" and it lists the errors and heresies, among them, of course, Popery, as Catholicism was commonly known. While rejecting variations on the Christian faith as unacceptable this document argues that man should have the liberty to worship God in the manner he chooses. Market Lavington's congregation and churchmen did not sign the letter but 81 other Wiltshire churches did so, among them Urchfont.

The opposition to non-conformism was certainly vehement and all the resources of civil and religious law and the courts were brought to bear on dissenters. Among the first of these to demand a separate religious ritual were the Society of Friends, the Quakers, and they were hounded cruelly and ruthlessly for more than half a century. Some were gaoled for refusing to pay the tithes ordered by the established church, while others refused to take an oath of allegiance, on the grounds that they would not swear an oath on any grounds and many more were fined the 12 pence a week for refusing to attend service in the local church. One supporter summed up the Quaker's dilemma by saying that "perpetually assured by the preachers of his party that it was unlawful to contribute money towards the maintenance of error, and being unskilled in the modern methods of meeting the enemy half-way, he just laid himself open to be systematically pillaged and ruined by any clerical, legal or municipal harpy who found pleasure in striking the unresistant. "

The Quakers were widespread and well organised by the mid-17th century and they were strong in Market Lavington, coinciding with the appearance in Wiltshire of two prominent dissenters, George Fox and William Penn. Fox visited Oare, near Pewsey, then Tetbury and Marlborough to encourage the faithful in 1656 and the authorities were quick to act. Within a few months, Thomas Withers of Bishops Cannings was apprehended in Market Lavington by John Jones, the village constable, who dragged him into an alehouse where he was held until the next morning, then sent to the county gaol where he was charged with making contact with other Quakers. Two neighbours paid his bail, but at the Assizes later in the year he was sentenced to six years imprisonment and his bailers were made to pay costs of £18. Withers contact was almost certainly with one of three Market Lavington families: the Gyes, the Selfes and the Axfords. The persecution of Isaac and Jane Selfe, leaders of the Quaker group in Market Lavington began in 1658, by which time Market Lavington's meeting of Friends had satellite groups in the Cheverells, Urchfont, Easterton and West Lavington. Selfe was arrested in 1660 on the word of the local layman in charge of the collection of tithes, John Merewether, who claimed that Selfe owed £40 in back tithes. He was gaoled in 1660, for six years, for refusing, on religious grounds, to pay the tithes. That same year William Bartlett of Market Lavington refused to pay one shilling and sixpence in tithes and was sent to gaol, where he died.

In 1663 Edward Gye and John Smith went to prison for nine weeks for refusing to pay a two pound fine[35] and in 1664 Robert Britton was arrested at a Market Lavington meeting of Quakers and imprisoned for eight years. Isaac Selfe was gaoled again in 1670 for holding a meeting in his house and for refusing to attend church, and while he was in gaol Jane Selfe, his wife, was imprisoned for holding meetings. At the same time the Selfe's household goods were seized and four Quakers who had been attending the meeting, Isaac Selfe junior, Edward Luffe and his son John, and Robert Foote of Comerwell, had goods appropriated. The bailiffs broke down the front door of Luffe junior's

house and seized three pairs of his shoes, valued at ten shillings, presumably the only items of value they could find, but Foote lost four oxen and two cows, valued at £32.

There was some amelioration in the lot of the Quakers after 1671, following a declaration of indulgence, or pardon, issued by Charles II and among those released were Edward Gye, Isaac Selfe and his wife, but the persecution continued, especially after the so-called Popish Plot of 1678. By that time there were 24 dissenters in the parish and almost certainly these were Quakers, and by 1682 they were obtaining significant local support and recognition. Henry Chivers, who was to build Clyffe Hall, joined two other justices of the peace in 1682 in writing to the King certifying that various Wiltshire Quakers were incorrectly being persecuted as Popish recusants. Nevertheless, at the time of the King's death in 1685, there were 34 Quakers in Wiltshire gaols and the Lavington Monthly Meeting, formed about 1680, took some risks initially.

The Lavington Meeting continued for 95 years, largely because the Toleration Act of 1689 put an end to persecution of all dissenters by removing from the established church the monopoly of legal forms of religious worship. In January 1690 the much-persecuted Isaac Selfe was holding regular meetings in his house and by 1716 the Quakers had erected a house for meetings - a House of Friends. Attending the first gathering were, apart from Selfe: John Gye, Edward Gye and William Miell. Meanwhile the Friends' numbers had been in decline in the early 18th century and the Salisbury Friends had joined the Lavington Monthly Meeting. The decline was steep after the cessation of the Lavington Monthly Meeting in 1775 and by 1790 there were only three Quakers in the parish. In 1799 the meeting-house was sold.

Today, with a small graveyard in front of it, it stands on the north side of High Street at right angles to the road. Though the Quakers were accepted, there was occasional animosity. At the beginning of the 19th century cottages in Parsonage Lane, near the High Street cross-roads, were the scene of great and unneighbourly hostility because in one cottage there lived a Quaker family. The persecution forced them to move to White Street.

The first *registered* non-established church religious meeting in the village was on 30 July 1689, when a chandler, Thomas Plank, possibly a Presbyterian, met with friends in his house. Other religious bodies were not registered until the late 18th century. Independents met at the house of William Smith in 1794, Smith being the only one attending who

---

[35] "Edward Gye and John Smith, being at a meeting of ye Peaple called Quakers at the house of Isaac Self in Lavington, were by John James, Constable, and other rude fellows taken and brought before Richard Lewis, who committed them to prison, where they were badly used and lay amongst felons, by whom Edward Gye had his cloathes stript from his back to his shirt."

had to make his mark instead of his signature. As the years passed and tolerance grew, so did the confidence of those outside the establishment.

An early convert to Methodism was David Saunders (1726-1796), known as the Pious Shepherd of Salisbury Plain, who, as a young man, earning six shillings and three pence a week as a Salisbury Plain shepherd, walked from his father's tiny cottage (long since gone) near the top of Russell Lane, Littleton Panell, to Devizes, to hear John Wesley preach. Saunders was quoted as saying in later life that neighbouring villages in those days were "sinks of iniquity" in which religion had "a very small place in the lives of the people." Presumably because of this, he resolved to devote the rest of his life to preaching the gospel as he understood Wesley to have taught it. He had no church or regular meeting-house, but he often said that over the years he had carried the word of God into every home in neighbouring villages - particularly in Market Lavington. He also built a shelter on the Plain for shepherds and shepherdesses, and he read the Bible to them there in stormy weather. It does not appear he profited from his labours, except for one £10 legacy bequeathed him late in life. There was more than one selfless soul in that impoverished family. Saunders' wife, Lydia, who died in 1785, aged 49, brought up 16 children over 20 years, burying four, while her husband preached his gospel. Perhaps those admirers mentioned on Saunders' gravestone, those "Christians in Europe, Asia, Africa and America," should have saved some admiration for Lydia.

In 1817 a group of Independents informed the authorities that "we do intend occasionally to use a house called the school-rooms in the centre of Market Lavington, consisting of two large rooms." Listed first among those attending was Amram Saunders (1779-1849) of Russell Mill, Littleton Panell, one of the more respected gentlemen of the neighbourhood and who, with his son, became spokesmen for the village in time of stress. The prime mover in this venture was Amram's sister, Elizabeth Saunders, who saw the opportunity for a Chapel Sunday school.[36] The house "with two large rooms" did, in fact, have several more. It was Parsonage House, in Parsonage Lane, and Elizabeth's Sunday school was partly, it seems, a reaction against the "vast amount of conviviality and riotous living" among the farmers, including her own father Amram, who "liked a game of cards and a glass of wine, and the squires and gentlemen of the place thought him a great acquisition to a hunting or card party." Amram saw the error of his ways, however, and "left the church,[37] renounced forever the hunting and card parties, made his bow to the squires and went to the meeting house - the Lower Meeting House." The family would drive by cart the mile and a quarter from Littleton Panell to Market Lavington - passing through three turnpike gates (these were burned in 1825) - before parking the cart in the "Green Dragon" yard and walking to the chapel from there. For many years Amram spent £40 to £50 a year on helping to maintain the chapel - there not being too many others who could afford to do so. Later he took over the superintendence of his sister's Sunday school - for 40 years.[38]

Catholics searched long and hard for a place of worship in Market Lavington and they celebrated Mass in curious surroundings at times. Until 1933 there was no place of worship for them in the village and many made the then arduous and expensive trip to Devizes on Sundays. In 1932 the village-born Joseph Sainsbury, himself a convert to Catholicism, returned from life in London with his German-born wife, Meta, and their four children, and he soon recognised that a church or at least a place of worship was needed. He built an extension to his house "The Retreat" and until 1940, a priest from Devizes, Father Louis Valluet, said Sunday Mass. Early in the Second World War soldiers swelled the congregation and Sainsbury moved the services to "Fives Court" in Parsonage Road, Market Lavington, sometimes to the village hall and later to the Sports Club in West Lavington. A service in 1943 at "Fives Court" is especially remembered because Italian prisoners-of-war who had been attending services, took charge of the Christmas decorations. They built an altar, altar rails and a manger scene with figures made from Lavington Hill clay. Old cocoa tins were adapted for candles and the prisoners-of-war sang Italian carols.

The Reverend Robert Sloper (died 1818) fostered Congregationalism in the parish. About 1805 nine people formed themselves into a church under his guidance and soon after they opened a Sunday school

---

[36] Her admiring neice Anne gives a vivid, though unintentionally unflattering, portrait of her: "The compressed, determined mouth, at once gave an idea of what she was capable; and to the end of her days, when she was sitting at chapel, or reading her Bible, or engaged in any devotional exercise, she had a persistent look, as if she was doing it in spite of somebody."

[37] The Parish records show that in March 1853 he informed the vestry that "henceforth he would refuse to pay all Church rates, and begged the policeman and not the collector might call upon him, when a rate was to be collected."

[38] Amram Saunders died in January 1849, in his then home, in Bath. His funeral by horse-drawn hearse, was followed by mourning coaches to Lavington. His daughter wrote that: "His old neighbours in Lavington closed their shops and, with a large party of Sunday School children, came out upon the highway and fell into the procession. They forgot his faults, remembered only his fine qualities, and followed him with many tears to his long home."

for boys in the bakehouse of Mr Gauntlet, as well as a "seminary for young ladies." The schools moved when they bought the former Quaker meeting-house as their chapel and enlarged it. The first pastor, Richard Ward, was recognised in 1809, and the chapel was enlarged and a gallery added.

On Census Sunday 1851, 220 attended morning service and 300 in the evening, but appropriate music, of all things, created problems. Much attention was given to the choir and there were unfavourable votes against the introduction of an organ. In 1852 a bass viol and two flutes joined the choir but in 1854 the congregation voted overwhelmingly for an organ. Even with this expense the church was fast approaching solvency.

The Market Lavington Congregationalists joined in the hundredth anniversary of the founding of Sunday schools in 1880 and more than a hundred children from Market Lavington went by wagons, drawn by a heavy traction engine, to celebrations at Devizes. The whole train was decorated with flowers from the countryside. A man carrying a red flag preceded the road train, moving at two miles an hour.

The Congregationalists built a new chapel on the opposite side of the road in 1892, at a cost of £653, and it had its own minister and services were held regularly. Electricity was installed in 1931.

Strict Baptists formed a church in the village in 1832, and in 1851 there were 50 present in the morning and 40 in the evening on Census Sunday. The chapel closed early this century and the building in Chapel Lane was converted into a fried-fish shop which is still in business. There is an adjoining graveyard.

BOUVERIES AND OTHERS

The Earls of Abingdon held the Manor of Lavington Rector for 72 years - until in 1764 the estates of Willoughby Bertie, fourth Earl of Abingdon (1740-1799), were put up for sale. One wonders whether the remarkable Bertie, "one of the most steady and intrepid assertors of liberty of his age," as one historian has called him, spent any of his younger years in his Wiltshire domain.

While the Abingdons were still lords of the manor, the family of Vince, who already had holdings in north Wiltshire, expressed interest in acquiring property in the neighbourhood. It is unclear when the family decided to settle in Market Lavington, but Henry Chivers Vince, the son of Frances Chivers and Henry Vince, acquired from Sir Edward des Bouverie about 20 acres at the south-western extremity of the village and built Clyffe Hall. Henry styled himself lord of the manors of Sevington in Leigh Delamere and of Fiddington in Gloucestershire. He died in 1748 and his widow died at Clyffe Hall in 1752. The property was deeply in debt by then[39] and for some years the Hall was leased out.

At the time of the 1764 sale of the Abingdon holdings in Market Lavington to the then London based family of Bouverie, Rector's Farm, presumably centred on the Old House, comprised more than 300 acres. It was under lease to Richard Legge at the time of the sale and the Bouveries soon acquired other acreage and properties, including, in 1814, Clyffe Hall.[40]

Inevitably the history of Market Lavington is tied to the Bouveries, but their arrival on the scene came at least six hundred years after the first Norman settlement in the village and their imprint, though generally benign, was primarily self-serving. Manorial estates were prime investments in the 17th and 18th centuries and the Bouveries made money from their many tenants, including the people of Market Lavington.

The family came from the Low Countries in the 16th century to escape the anti-Protestant pogroms of the Duke of Alba. The first Bouverie we know of, Laurens, was born near Lille, fled to Frankfurt where he became an accountant to a merchant, whose daughter he married. At the age of 32, in 1568, he settled in Canterbury and 36 years later he moved to London. His son, Edward, was knighted and his christening cup, entitled "Fortune's Boat," is still part of the family silver. The traditional toast in it is "Health and prosperity, peace and prosperity, long life and fellowship and the joys of eternity" - an obeisance to materialism and a nod to the spiritual life.

In the last quarter of the 17th century Sir Edward des Bouverie acquired the estate of Little Cheverell and he had a house there, just to the south-west of the church. Sir Edward's son, Sir William, was knighted in 1713 and made a baronet in 1714. His son, Sir Edward,

---

[39] Henry Vince had expensive tastes - in furniture at least. A bill from a warehouse in Frith Street, Soho, in 1738, shows he spent £8 18s. on a walnut desk and bookcase and £9 9s. on a carved and gilt "eagle" table - to mention only a few items. These prices are on a par with those being paid for 16th and 17th century oak furniture at the sale of the contents of the Awdrey manor in Market Lavington nearly 200 years later.

[40] In a memoir written in 1930 Edward Oliver Pleydell Bouverie (1853-1936) explains his forebears interest in property thus: "......at this date an individual who was not in trade had but little scope for investing any money that he did not wish to spend. If he wished to trade he practically had to become a partner in the business with its liabilities and drawbacks. Chartered companies, it is true, did exist but the public companies were few, and companies consisting of shares with a limited liability were a creation of Victorian times. It would be natural then that a man who could afford it would buy land and if he could do so at the same time increasing the boundary of an estate which he then owned he would naturally prefer to do so."

Clyffe Hall during the early 1920's.

The 'bag' of hares and partridges after a day's shooting on Knap Farm, early in the century.
Standing at the rear of the game cart is 'Shep' Perry who had a dual role: shepherd and gamekeeper.

Mr Ross, head gardener at Clyffe Hall, standing in his garden at the gardener's cottage (now 41 The Spring), in the early 1920's.

bought Longford Castle in 1717. Because he died childless the property passed to his brother Jacob. Jacob married Mary Clarke, an heiress, had a family of 13, and made a fortune in trade with Turkey. In 1736 the family changed its name to Bouverie and, having found fortune, sought honours that only the Court could bestow. In this the Bouveries were assisted by the mistress of George II, in 1747, for a fee of £12,000.

Finally the Barons Bouverie, became the Earls of Radnor. The second Viscount, William Bouverie, married to good advantage twice - firstly to Harriet, only daughter of Sir Mark Pleydell, and heiress to Coleshill; and secondly to Rebecca Alleyne, a Barbadian heiress. He became the first Earl Radnor in 1761 and the family motto, acquired along the way, was: "the fatherland is dear but liberty is dearer." Money was left out of the equation, there being at this stage more than enough of it - and sometimes it was put to good use. Thus the second Earl, Jacob, built the Council Chamber at Salisbury, at a cost of £10,000, when the old one was burnt down.

"CHARITY" AND CHARITIES

A temporary and partial alleviation of poverty for many was to "go on the Parish" - a form of dole. The Parish Commissioners distributed coal, meat, corn, clothes and blankets as they saw fit. Their records in the 18th century show there were many and varied demands on the parish purse. The so-called Poor Account, begun in 1727, provided money for burials, for tending to smallpox patients, for the maintenance of illegitimate children, for "looking after ye Parish poorhouse for one year - £3 3s. 0d.," for attendance at the court, for apprentices, for vagrants and for workhouse rent. There were also sundry obscure items, such as "cloth for James Giddins boys cloos," and "Edward Gye's bill for hosen - a shilling and ten pence." Some charges were surprisingly high. In 1736 three guineas to the doctor "for Elizabeth Wheeler's fingar," seems extortionate. A few years later John Giddins' coffin cost the parish only eight shillings.

In the next century money went regularly to illegitimate children - one shilling and sixpence a week was a typical rate in 1802 - and to the families of militia men in camps outside the county or called abroad.

There were also philanthropists which gave cash to the most needy. Market Lavington had several of these and it still has. Today the sums involved seem small, but they were not so two hundred years ago. At the time of a bequest of £200 to the parish, in 1733, by St Asaph's Bishop, Thomas Tanner, a labourer's wage was no more than £7 a year. Tanner, the son of a Market Lavington vicar from 1671 to 1719, was born at the Old Parsonage in Parsonage Lane in 1673. His chief claim to fame rests on a work which he supposedly wrote when he was barely 20 called *A Short Notice on the Religious Houses of England and Wales*. He visited Market Lavington several times later in his life; at least once, according to tradition, "in a coach with purple lines and mitres on the sides." His bequest details are on a tablet in the bell-tower of St Mary's. He asked that the observance of his charity should be on St Paul's Day every January and that bells be rung for a service in the afternoon, after which the trustees should spend 20 shillings "at a friendly meeting to which they are to invite such of the better sort of Parishioners.....to promote peace and good neighbourhood and preserve some little regard to the memory of the Bishop's honoured parents." The charity has survived, and the Green Dragon has been occasionally the scene of Tanner's good-neighbourly gather, where in times past the memory of the Bishop was drunk from a punchbowl. Tanner's charity still produces a small annual income but no feast has been held since 1966.

Another benefactor was Thomas Sainsbury and his brother William, who by their wills dated 1795 and 1796, bequeathed £200 each to invest for the poor of the parish. The wills say specifically that the interest arising from the money should be paid to the minister and church wardens "for the time being to be by them laid out in the purchase of bread to be distributed to the most necessitous poor of the parish of Market Lavington on Easter and Christmas Even every year." 668 loaves were given away in 1833 to about 160 heads of families and single people in the parish, and in 1845 Maria Sainsbury added another £200 to the charity's capital. At the beginning of this century the income from the three Sainsbury charities, then amounting to £16 annually, was spent on bread and groceries for the needy, and in 1972 bread vouchers amounting to about £28 were given away. There have been distributions occasionally since then.

In an 1865 will Thomas and Sarah Stobbert bequeathed £400 to provide coal for all poor widows and widowers aged more than 50 on Christmas Eve. Each recipient was to receive one and a half hundred-weight of coal.

Yet another charity was provided by a Great Cheverell resident, James Townsend, who, by his 1725 will, bequeathed to the Market Lavington parish 40 shillings annually to buy "2 cloth coats of a grey colour and 2 hats for the use of 2 such poor men of the said parish as had no relief of the said parish, or to buy clothes therewith for two such poor women of the said parish.....to be delivered to them on St Thomas's Day yearly."

An unusual and none too well documented charity involved a number of so-called parish chairs. These were purchased with surplus money from Queen Victoria's Jubilee festivities and they were lent out to the aged and sick at the request of the vicar or doctors. The Parish Council did not have custody of the chairs and, inevitably, some of them disappeared.

"TO TROUBLE ME TO BURY HER"

There is always one good village story and Market

Lavington's is recounted by none other than Lavington's true gentleman and historian par excellence, Edward Oliver Pleydell Bouverie, of the Old House. It concerns a curate with a reputation for violence. The curate was a Welshman, reportedly "of drunken habits," named Williams, who was in charge of day to day affairs of the church in the absence of the long-serving Rector, John Dobson, who lived at Longbridge Deverill. There had been a smallpox outbreak in the neighbourhood in 1785 and tempers were understandably short. Involved with Williams was the overseer of Eastcott Farm, named Axford, who was certainly related to the tragic Axford family of Eastcott whose memorial tablet is in St Mary's Church. Axford said in deposition taken after his encounter with Williams that he applied to the curate to bury a smallpox victim, a female parishioner, in St Mary's churchyard and Williams appeared to agree. But later, when Axford presented himself with the corpse at the churchyard he found the gate locked. Axford then sought out Williams at Dr Chandler's house in the Market Place. According to Axford, Williams told him "What business hast thee to bring that woman out of thy parish into mine to trouble me to bury her?" Axford said he wished to keep smallpox away from Eastcott as Williams had done on other occasions in Market Lavington. To this Williams replied "In a great passion he said I was a Damned dirty fellow for so doing; which made me examine my cloathes all over and found nothing Dirty but my shoes and I then told the parson if he would give me leave to clean my shoes I thought I should be as clean as he was."

Williams was adamant, however, and said he would not bury the corpse unless he received six shillings and eight pence. Axford refused to pay and Williams then began abusing him. As the overseer turned to walk down four steps into the Market Place "I felt a terrible Blow in my head which struck me down and then before I could recover myself the Parson had struck me down again. He then got astride me and took my hair in one hand and with his fist he beat me in a terrible manner. I then arose and found the blood running out of my ears, mouth and nose, with my Waistcoat and shirt Tore very much. I then took up a stick and struck him three times in the side."

Much shouting followed and Axford reminded the Parson that "When he came into Wiltshire in some old yarn stockings," he was obliged to everyone who "would supply him with a dinner but now having married an old maid[41] just going into her grave, and he to inherit from her between £8,000 and £10,000, he no longer bothered to curry friendships."

So concerned was Axford to have the corpse buried that he paid Williams the six shillings and eight pence, but the feud did not end. Axford reported that he could not go to service on most Sundays "without being called to order without any cause, especially Christmas Day last when we rose to very high words in the church to the great detriment of the service." This last remark suggests a degree of informality, to put it mildly, in the way church services were conducted - at least when Parson Williams was in the pulpit.

There is a curious footnote to this story. In the same century as Axford's confrontation with Williams, a certain Mr Axford lived in Littleton Pannell, in a tall, red-brick house of the early Georgian period, on the opposite side of the road from the village church. The vicar, whose name goes unrecorded, wanted very much to have Axford's house as his vicarage but Axford, according to a contemporary report, "had taken a particular dislike to the vicar and he willed solemnly that the vicar should never possess the house," while he, Axford, and his wife were alive. The wife died but, "with great determination," Axford lived to be 90. When he felt his end to be near, and the parson was closing in for the kill, so to speak, he married his serving girl, aged 20, thereby ensuring that the house would remain in private hands. Could this have been the same Axford, who had good reason to steer clear of some churchmen? It is possible. His confrontation with the awful Welshman was well within the life-span of the long-lived Littleton Pannell Axford.

It is not the only record, however, of churchmen turning away bodies for burial. The Parish records show that as recently as 1849 the vicar refused to perform burial services for deceased parishioners, apparently because they had sought religious advice or instruction elsewhere. It is encouraging to report that the churchwardens overruled him.

HEALTH

The concern of Williams for the spread of smallpox in Market Lavington, in 1785, was understandable. It was endemic in England in the 18th century and eight people died from smallpox in the village in 1799. In fact Market Lavington was lucky to escape so lightly.

It appears, however, that it did not escape in 1721, when St Mary's Parish Register shows that 104 people were buried. Presumably some of these died of smallpox as in an average year at that time there were 15 burials. In a three month period in mid-1721 five members of the Kill family were buried and the Parish records for 1728 note that both William Sainsbury and his wife had the disease. In Salisbury in 1723 it reached epidemic proportions with 1244 cases, and 165 died, while in Calne in 1731 there were 176 deaths.

Infectious diseases were rarely understood and others like "consumption" (tuberculosis), "fever", dropsy, measles and "convulsions" listed in the Parish records as the chief causes of death, took a terrible toll in the rural community.[42] Interestingly, the records make no mention of our two modern scourges - heart

---

[41] A member the Sainsbury family, according to one report.

Fiddington House, circa 1912.
The house and grounds occupied the Hamilton Drive, Fiddington Place and Stirling Road areas.

Market Lavington Manor, circa 1900.
It was built in 1865 by the Pleydell Bouveries and since 1928 has been owned by Dauntsey's School.

disease and cancer. Two men died of "The Evil," which was tuberculosis of the lymph glands, an obsolete disease in Britain today. There was an epidemic of measles in 1790, which killed 11 children under five, and five children died of the "cruppe" (whooping cough) in 1811. Cholera was another killer and in the 1849 epidemic in Devizes 67 people died.

The old barn abutting the road at the top of Parsonage Lane and now part of Barn Hill House, was fitted out as a hospital for smallpox in the epidemic of 1873, but it was not used because the epidemic suddenly abated. The bodies were not taken into the church at the time but the vicar who visited the sick died of the disease himself.

The transcripts of burials in the 18th century make grim and revealing reading and are a stark reminder of the hard life and sombre circumstances of death for many. Thus an unnamed "travelling woman" died on 8 February 1740 "by the inclemency of weather." There appears to have been no room at the inn for her. There were many "buried from the workhouse" and many more "buried from the poorhouse" - four in 1786 alone. There is one especially pathetic entry, noting the death of one workhouse inmate, the four-day-old Matilda Godden.[43]

There was another malady which, though not by any means fully understood, did receive attention of a sort. This was mental illness, and people from west Wiltshire and neighbouring counties paid to become inmates in the private asylum which Robert Willett set up in Market Lavington in 1816. He was a partner, with one Valentine Leach, in a Devizes drapery firm in The Brittox. Willett had read of an institution in Heslington, outside York, begun in 1796 by the Society of Friends, for "persons whose circumstances enabled them to pay for a pleasant home in cheerful surroundings," as the Devizes Gazette reported many years later.[44]

Precisely why Willett chose Market Lavington for his money-making idea is unclear, but he opened his establishment in the heart of the village, in the High Street. He was already advertising in the Devizes Gazette on 27 March 1817 that his establishment was "pleasantly situated with several acres of grounds appropriate to horticultural pursuits calculated to induce the patients to take bodily exercise." Families of patients were advised to contact Dr Headley, of Devizes, who was physician to the institution, or Mr Box, of Lavington, a surgeon, who had some connection with Willett. The several acres referred to must have been an extension of the gardens of the village house.

The asylum was a successful business venture except that the residents of the High Street complained that the inmates were noisy. For this reason and because he also needed more space Willett bought and moved into Fiddington Hill Farm or Fiddington House in 1834. The move did nothing to reduce the mortality rate at the asylum, however. There are no figures for the early years - from 1817 to 1825, but in 1827 there were four deaths, 1828 three, 1829 four, 1830 two, 1831 five, 1832 three, 1835 five, 1836 six and 1837, the last year recorded, seven. That is 41 deaths in 11 years. Clearly the larger establishment, with its 15 acres "of plantation and pasture" and its "apartments and airing grounds as to suit the different classes of patients, maintaining those distinctions desirable according to circumstances of life," (another Devizes Gazette advertisement) added to the enrolment, the income and, inevitably, to the death toll. Willett was assisted by his son and partner, by then Dr John Willett, from 1842 and another doctor joined the staff later. The 1841 Census shows that by then the Fiddington House asylum had 170 private patients - 100 women and 70 men - under the care of Willett, aged 60, his son, John, the "residing physician," four nurses[45] and a housekeeper. Four other servants listed took care of the Willett father and son and Willett's wife, presumably. So, five were in charge of 170 and four ministered to the needs of three. The cook must have cooked for all and must have been very busy indeed.[46]

The Willetts sold out before 1851 and the asylum obtained state assistance by taking in "pauper" patients.

[42] It was not until the 1860s that real attempts were made to eradicate infectious diseases in rural communities and the changes were prompted by a series of outbreaks of diphtheria, typhus and cholera, with many deaths among the rural poor. The impression remains that local authorities became interested only when the epidemics showed signs of spreading in the community as a whole.

[43] Babies and infants were taken into the workhouse and separated from their mothers and about a third of these children died each year. In some instances the aged, the infirm or even the feeble-minded, were put to care for the babies. A Royal Commission on workhouse conditions published as late as 1905-1909 found that 14,000 children under 16 were in general mixed workhouses in England which also housed a large lunatic and idiot population as well as the sick and the aged. Here is an extract from the Commission's report: "We have seen imbeciles annoying the sane, and the sane tormenting the imbeciles. We have seen half-witted women nursing the sick, feeble-minded women in charge of the babies, and imbecile old men put to look after the boys out of school hours."

[44] Willett could have presented himself, with justice, as a benefactor because the county lunatic asylums were always full. The alternative was the workhouse or private nursing - for those who could afford it and take the strain. He was, in fact, doing a job nobody else wanted to do - for a price.

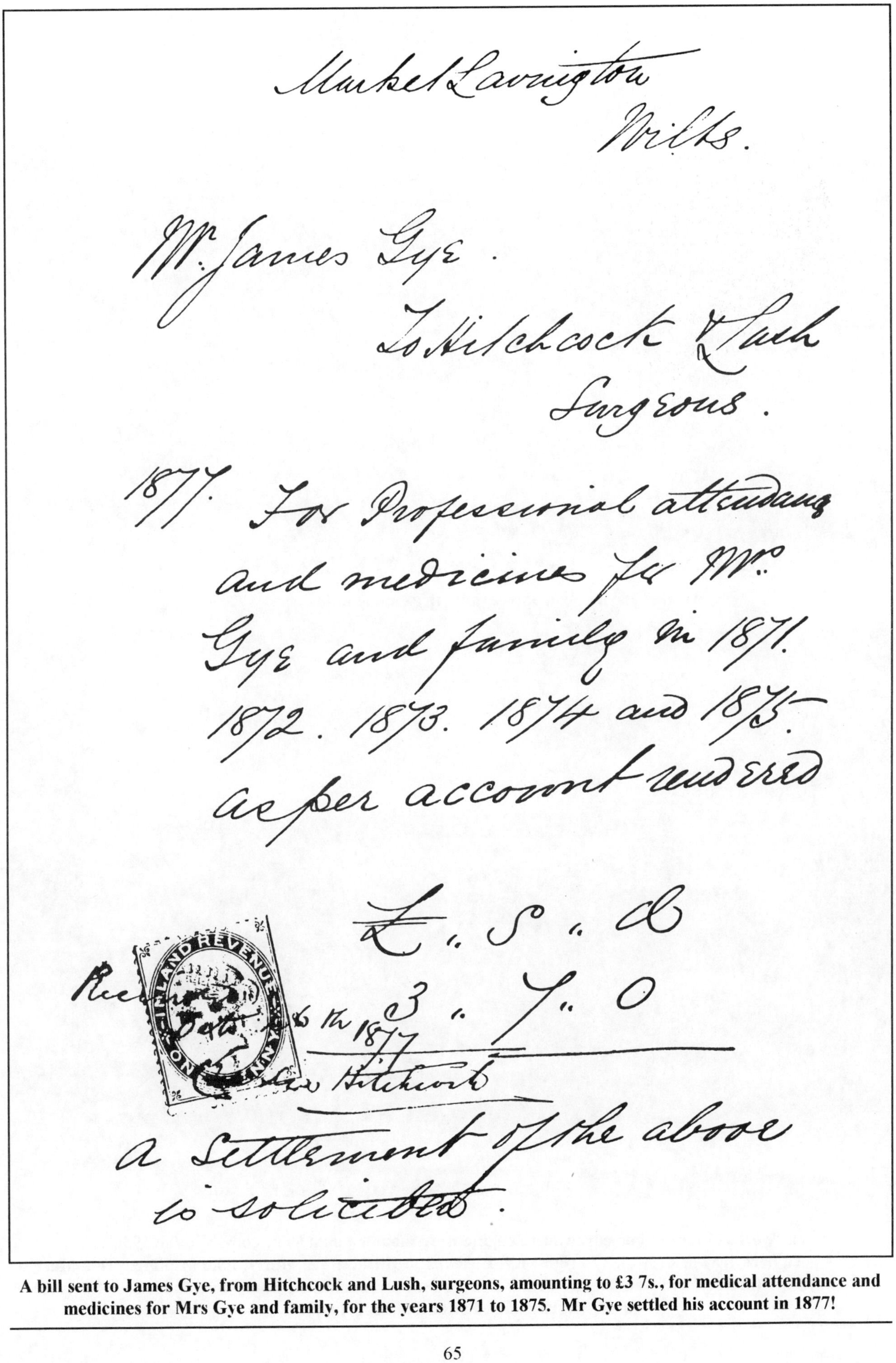

Market Lavington
Wilts.

Mr James Gye.

To Hitchcock & Lush
Surgeons.

1877.   For Professional attendance
and medicines for Mrs.
Gye and family in 1871.
1872. 1873. 1874 and 1875.
as per account rendered

£ . S . d

Received 6th 1877   3 . 7 . 0

Geo Hitchcock

A Settlement of the above
is solicited.

A bill sent to James Gye, from Hitchcock and Lush, surgeons, amounting to £3 7s., for medical attendance and medicines for Mrs Gye and family, for the years 1871 to 1875. Mr Gye settled his account in 1877!

Market Lavington's horsedrawn fire engine in the early 1920's.

The works of the old horsedrawn fire engine were mounted on a lorry chassis in the 1930's.
The crew seen here are back row, left to right: Bill Elisha, Jim Hurkett, Alf Merritt, Sid Mullings, Tom Merritt,
Bob Milsom (driver); and standing are Frank George (at rear, engineer), Harry Buckland, Jack Saxton,
Jack Merritt, Jack Potter and Ron Huxtable.

The new proprietor was Charles Hitchcock, described as a "surgeon and apothecary," and he was aged 39. Living on the premises was another "surgeon and apothecary John Ives, Hitchock's son and three daughters, seven nurses and two assistants." There were 103 "pauper" patients[47] and 40 private. Hitchcock hung on and at the age of 79, in 1891, was still in charge. By then he had acquired another wife, who lived with him, plus a niece and six grandsons. There were six attendants for the 15 private patients still remaining.

The *Devizes Gazette,* from the safety of a later date, detected something unsavoury about Willett's early venture when it noted that the son of Willett's partner, Leach, "took his first step on the ladder of fortune" by establishing a lunatic asylum, as his father-in-law had done. This he did in Wales and so successful was he that he returned to Devizes with a large fortune - large enough to take over the "proprietorship," as the *Devizes Gazette* put it, of Devizes Castle. The *Devizes Gazette* adds that the fortune came not from lunacy but from certain other "operations" in Wales, but the implication remains that there was profit to be made out of terrible misfortune.

Market Lavington was not, however, an unhealthy place by the standards of the time, and in 1875 a local newspaper article claimed that there were few places in Wiltshire healthier. It based this claim on figures for burials from 1818 to 1836. In that period 496 were buried, of whom 36 were aged 80 to 90 years old, 78 from 70 to 80, and 55 from 60 to 70. What is just as interesting about the figures is the infant mortality. No less than 64 died aged under one year, and 95 died between the ages of one and 20. Not much better are the figures for the 20 to 40 age group (72) and for the 40 to 60 group (80). So the village appears, on the basis of these not entirely convincing statistics, to have been healthy for the elderly yes, but for the young and middle-aged, not so healthy.

One of the early curers of ills, whose surgery in Market Lavington was the street outside his home, was Dr Batter, an 18th century herb-doctor. Described as a genuine old-fashioned specimen of his class, Batter had humble origins and lived and dressed as a poor man in a roadside cottage where his grandfather had lived before him. His patients' waiting room was the hedge-bank and he would usually prescribe plants from the neighbourhood.

LAWBREAKERS

The frustrations of a hard existence and life-long poverty in some cases were prime causes of petty law-breaking in rural communities. It is surprising, in fact, that there was not more serious crime. In the rural communities in earlier centuries the working man's relief from the daily grind of existence was often alcohol. Market Lavington had more publicans - eight - in 1620 than it did three hundred years later and they served not only beer, but claret, sack and aqua vitae (raw spirit). In 1830 the village had six public houses (the Angel, the Bell, the Green Dragon - which was a posting house and an excise office - the Kings Arms, the New Inn and, at Easterton, the Royal Oak). In addition it had a beer retailer, William Oxford, and five maltsters or brewers.

Drunkenness was a misdemeanour, punishable by a fine or, if repeated often, by a cooling-off period in the lock-up. It was not regarded as seriously as was swearing, particularly under the Commonwealth, chiefly because swearing then was considered of a religious nature - "the taking of oaths." Constables and magistrates having to mete out punishment were often the targets of remarkably inventive oaths - thereby adding to the sentence of the oath-taker.[48] Punishment varied. Under the Profane Oaths Act of 1745 fines were graded according to status and, presumably, income. Labourers, soldiers, sailors and seamen were fined a shilling, others under the degree of gentleman two shillings and all those above that degree were fined five shillings. The fine was to be paid at once or the

---

[45] Nurses then were not trained as they were a hundred years later. One report speaks of them being slovenly and ignorant and often feeble-minded if they were nursing paupers. This is not to suggest that Willett's staff fitted that description, but the fact remains that late in the 19th century the feebleminded could still be seen in workhouses helping to nurse the sick and the insane and were considered a step lower on the scale of need than the merely physically ill.

[46] The Lunacy Amendment Act which called for the creation of well and suitably equipped awards for the housing of the mentally unfit did not come into force until 1862 and even then the local authorities refused to avail themselves of the Act.

[47] In 1867, a report on public asylums in Wiltshire said that a mortality rate of 11.7 per cent at these asylums was far less than the mortality which formerly prevailed "when the unhappy pauper lunatics were huddled together in private asylums, in wretched dens with barely sufficient respiration."

[48] Witnesses said that one Pewsey Vale resident delivered himself of more than 40 oaths without repeating himself, but the undisputed master of swearing appears to have been William Morgan of Turlowe in Bradford on Avon, who was arrested for uttering 120 profane curses. We can only wonder who counted them.

offender spent ten days in gaol. Women, known as "scolds" if they had a mind to strong language, were occasionally "ducked" - that is, sat in a "ducking-stool" and immersed in the local stream - in the case of Market Lavington, in Broadwell.

A minor offence which appeared early in Market Lavington's annals was "selling light." In 1607, for instance, Richard Luffe, the local baker was fined five shillings for having sold his twopenny black loaves three ounces light. And that year John Meryweather and Richard Hurle, both tradesmen in the village, were fined three shillings and fourpence each for not appearing with weights and measures for examination. An offence for which the punishments were much heavier - six months in gaol and confiscation of goods for a first offence - was "engrossing," what today we call cornering the market and selling for a profit. In 1615 four Market Lavington traders, Richard Crawley, Aldred Newton, John Hollowaye and Richard Hollowaye, were convicted for this offence because they had cornered the market not only on wheat, but also on rye, barley, malt, beans and peas.

During the reign of James I rabbit-poaching was the commonest serious offence for which Wiltshiremen were on trial and the offence was punishable, under some circumstances, by death. But James, who was both a bigot and a hypocrite, had other ways of hounding his subjects. His statute of 1620 demanded of every subject 40 days of Lenten fasting in which all were forbidden meat and beer at all times and were forbidden supper on Friday evenings. All inn-keepers, alehouse-keepers, taverners, butchers, grocers and restaurateurs (called in those days "keepers of ordinary tables") had to pay between £10 and £20 (say £2,000 to £4,000 in today's money), plus sureties of two bondsmen, not to sell prohibited products during Lent and if they refused to enter into this bond they were to be imprisoned. Market Lavington's seven inn-keepers and two butchers paid up, but one wonders what they did with their time and how they earned a living for nearly six weeks. And if Lavingtonians, like every one else, turned to fish six days a week - and every Friday for 45 weeks of the year - where did they get it?

A fruitful source of day-to-day living in Market Lavington in the 18th century are the *Notebooks of William Hunt*, a prosperous West Lavington country gentleman who became a compassionate magistrate. He kept a painstaking record of cases which came before him between 1744 and 1749. It was hardly a catalogue of rogues. The most common offences were assault and stealing wood; the woodstealers presumably were people needing to keep themselves warm. For his petty sessions hearing, Hunt favoured public houses. In Market Lavington he used the Green Dragon or the Bell, at West Lavington the Horse and Jockey, at Great Cheverell the Bell, and at Potterne the George.

Among the many people who took wood from more fortunate neighbours in the colder months was a

Betty -------, who stole kindling in the bitter month of February 1745. She was fined a shilling. Mary ----- was fined nine times that in December of the previous year for breaking down the boundaries of "farmer Holloway's field" and stealing his "hedgewood."

Less serious miscreants came before Hunt in September 1744. Before him were five boys accused by Ambrose Draper of Market Lavington of having robbed his orchard. The boys confessed and were fined two shillings each, the money to go to the poor and to Draper. Two shillings was several years' pocket money at that time.

Potentially much more serious but coming to nothing was the complaint of Rebecca -------, in August the same year, that a neighbouring parishioner had robbed and ravaged her. When he fled, Rebecca said he had not been the person responsible. Case closed.

In November the same year Phillip Sainsbury, of the well-known and respected family in the village, was accused by the village constable of having refused to assist him in the execution of his office. Justice Hunt offers no other details but he excused Sainsbury of punishment on his paying for the cost of the warrant and "acknowledging his fault before justices on his knees."

That same month Market Lavington parish officers issued a complaint against one John Peplar for not giving his wife maintenance. Hunt ordered him to pay her sixpence a week, "he being old and poor."

A complaint reflecting well on nobody came from the churchwardens and overseers of the poor of Market Lavington that a villager had begot "a bastard child or children on the body of a single woman." He appeared before Justice Hunt and his brother offered surety for him, but the case appears not to have been proceeded with. Accusations along these lines were not unusual in the 18th century and usually were settled out of court. In another similar case in Market Lavington an order was made against a man for maintenance of a child but the man promptly enlisted in the army and disappeared abroad.

Fines varied from as little as a few pence to as much as £10 - a very large sum. One man found guilty of assaulting a sheriff's bailiff spent six months in Devizes Gaol before his case came to court; because of this his fine was six pence.

A reminder that the Lord's day was still sacred came in the month of September 1745 when two Market Lavingtonians reported Joseph Boulter of Erlestoke for having "suffered tippling in his house." He had to pay ten shillings to the poor of the parish. Boulter was, apparently, a persistent offender and was soon selling beer and ale without a licence. A relative of his was an equally persistent offender, as we shall soon see.

Less grievous was the turnip-stealing of a Market Lavington resident, which Magistrate Hunt found "so trifling" that he arranged an agreement between the offender and the turnip-owner.

The word prostitution was not mentioned in Magistrate Hunt's notebooks but he did adjudicate on a case brought by two "credible witnesses" who reported that one Market Lavington parishioner had "entertained ten rogues or vagabonds" at her house. Hunt fined her 30 shillings.

Hunt's punishment for under-age offenders - whipping - appears severe in the late 20th century, but remember that stealing a loaf of bread was considered a capital offence in some English counties at the time. A whipping for two Market Lavington teenagers for cutting wood in the coppice of the then Lord of the manor, the Earl of Abingdon, was Hunt's way of warning them. Another common punishment was sentencing to the stocks for an hour or two. These were usually in the most public of places - in the case of Market Lavington, in the High Street for a time, but more commonly in the Market Place. A vicar, the Reverend Atley, remarked in 1855 that the Market Place was "a favourite resort of the juvenile portion of the population. The stocks have lost their dread and the clanking iron [has] become a musical instrument in their estimation."

Violence was not confined to villagers in Hunt's jurisdiction. At a Potterne sitting of the court, five women came before him for brawling in the churchyard on the Sabbath. He told them to behave themselves. He settled another dispute among three women who assaulted each other in the harvest fields above Market Lavington in August 1747. He dealt more severally with a Market Lavington woman accused of "cursing and swearing six oaths" in the Market Lavington Market Place, in July 1748, in the presence of William Sainsbury, the town clerk. Hunt ordered her to pay the fine, which she refused to do, so he sentenced her to ten days hard labour in Devizes Gaol.

A BRACE OF HIGHWAYMEN

Serious crime around Market Lavington and the Plain in recent centuries centred on highwaymen and the most famous of these was Thomas Boulter, who in his brief career held up and robbed more men and women than any highwayman in England in the 18th century (and possibly any other century). Boulter was born in Poulshot, near Devizes, and his associations with Market Lavington are through his uncle, Isaac

Blagden, a village resident. Boulter's father was also a highwayman of sorts[49] and both his father and mother were whipped publicly in Devizes Market Place - there is no record of the reason for his mother's punishment - while the younger Boulter was in his teens.[50] We are not concerned here with the career of Boulter the younger, though it does show how precarious was travel across the Plain in the 1770's. His uncle Isaac Blagden appears to have been type-cast for his role. A police circular described him as "a stout well-set man of a swarthy complexion..... very much pitted with the small pox, round visaged and rather stoops in his walk, about 32 years of age."

It appears his career was even briefer than his nephew's but he was very much more fortunate. He tried to rob a man a little way north of Market Lavington in 1775 and his victim was not only armed but ready to shoot. The man "lodged a brace of slugs" in Blagden's thigh and left him bleeding on the highway. He was remarkably lucky to escape gaol. Passers-by carried him into the village and friends there insisted that the parish authorities should take care of him and call a surgeon. The leg-wound was cured but Blagden carried a limp as long as he lived. The man he attacked refused to press the matter.

Three years later, when nephew Boulter was ranging far between Wiltshire and London, Blagden was arrested for a foolish remark at the Cross Keys public house at Fovant. He was drinking and talking about his nephew's exploits, and the price on his head, and was overheard to say that "I think we had better be off or we shall be advertised too." It was assumed that he was an accomplice of Boulter and he was again lucky to escape a gaol sentence. The following year Boulter absolved his uncle of any blame in his exploits at least by saying from his own prison cell that Blagden had never been a party to any of his robberies. Boulter was hanged in August 1778 after making an eloquent and well-reasoned plea for mercy[51] - he had not, in fact, killed anyone - and Blagden ended his days in the Lavington workhouse.

The old road from Lavington across the Plain was, of course, a prime target for less professional footpads than Blagden. One of the latest and certainly one of the most bungled highway hold-ups recorded in the area was in 1839, when a wealthy farmer of Imber was returning from Devizes fair via Market Lavington.

[49] Boulter senior was caught stealing a horse and selling it, and at the Winchester Assizes in 1775 he was condemned to death. His friends intervened and his sentence was commuted to 14 years transportation.

[50] A law abolishing the public flogging of women in England came into force in 1829.

[51] The *Wiltshire Independent* wrote many years later of Boulter's considerable mystique in these terms: "Whose was the phantom steed, invulnerable to steel, incapable of fatigue, who swept like a driven cloud across the startled village green, and whose fabulous powers of locomotion had, in the next instant of time, transported its rider to the distant hills, where the listeners might, perchance, hear the challenge of a bellowing blunderbuss, answered by the horseman's long laugh of defiance, fading into echoes along the Plain?" They don't write like that any more.

A 'Hospital Week' carnival procession from Easterton makes its way down the High Street in the mid 1920's.
By this time the premises of Briant's Restaurant, on the corner of the Market Place,
had become the London Joint City & Midland Bank.

Market Lavingtonians returning from a 1910 outing to the tea gardens at Edington. In the front cart are
members of the Hopkins family, suggesting that most of the trippers were members of the
Congregational Church and the Sunday School.

Four men pulled him from his horse and held him by the throat while they searched him. They took his horse but he managed to summon help and a band of locals led by a constable scoured the plain. They pursued three, one of whom fell dead from his exertions, and captured the other two. The fourth man was caught several days later; the surviving three were sentenced at Devizes to 14 years transportation.

AGRARIAN POVERTY

It is too easy to blame crime on poverty, but it often grew out of pent up anger and despair, particularly during the earlier part of the 19th century when the disenfranchised working masses had few ways of expressing their rejection of a seemingly indifferent system. Certainly the gentry paid little attention until the violence which ravaged southern England in the autumn of 1829 and the first months of 1830 brought near-revolution to their door. It was a timely reminder to the born-lucky that poverty is a disease which the community as a whole must cure.

It was an uprising of poverty-stricken land-workers which began in Kent and spread literally within days across the south. The seeds had long since been sown. William Cobbett reported from a tour of the Avon valley in 1826 that cattle, horses and other animals were better housed and fed than the agricultural labourers and their children. The Wiltshire labourers were "the worst used on the face of the earth," he said. It was, in fact, true that in the first third of the 19th century, Wiltshire was the most poverty-stricken county in England and in mid-century a sixth of the population was on relief which was withdrawn when any member of the household, including a seven year old, went to work.

A key factor in this scene of destitution was the "poor law" which grew out of the inflationary price of staple food. Grain prices nearly doubled in the latter quarter of the 18th century and if the labouring poor were not to die of starvation there were only two possible remedies for the government of the day. One was to raise their wage to a legal minimum and this the government, under pressure from the landed gentry, would not do. The other was to assist wages with cash payments financed from higher rates levied from those who were in a position to pay them. The Government introduced a so-called bread scale and brought pauper wages - to those on the parish dole - up to the point of their being able to buy so much bread and no more. As a result agricultural labourers' wages fell to the level of those paupers, and farmers turned for part-time work from parish labour which they could dismiss at any time. Inevitably, the agricultural worker went "on the parish" and often available labourers were auctioned like animals. This form of assistance to the poor via the imposition of higher rates also bankrupted many small employers.

The average weekly wage for an agrarian labourer in 1774 was five shillings a week, rising to six shillings in 1794. That wage would buy 14 loaves of bread for a family of four or five, but by 1815, when the wage had risen to seven and then to eight shillings a week, that income would buy only nine loaves. By 1828 the wage had fallen back to five shillings a week, making it lower than had been 34 years earlier. Many agrarian workers could not rely on work at any time of the year, even in harvest, because the pool of labour was so large and in harvest time those same wages were paid to men who worked a 17-hour day, from three o'clock in the morning on cutting the crop, and to women who worked the same hours, from two o'clock in the morning tying the sheaves. The only bonus these harvesters had was free alcohol, which may have helped them through the night. Working beside the adults and earning a few pence a day were their sons and daughters. As late as 1843, boys and girls were joining the labour force at the age of seven or eight, and by 1867 the average age for children beginning full-time work was nine - earlier than most other areas of England.[52]

GIVE THEM AN ACRE

It was these starving men and women[53] who in 1830 took to the fields, burned haystacks and barns and destroyed agricultural machinery which they believed, correctly, was replacing them. The unrest began in Kent in November and spread as suddenly as the fires it started. Men gathered in bands of a hundred and more, and ranged the countryside - some to protest, some to destroy and some to look on. Most were hungry.[54]

[52] The Wiltshire essayist on rural scenes, Richard Jeffries wrote in 1874 of the labourer's cottage: "The rain comes through the thatch, the mud floor is damp and perhaps sticky. The cold wind comes through the ill-fitting sash and drives with terrible force under the door..... The low chimneys smoke incessantly and fill the rooms with smother..... Here the family are all huddled together, close over the embers. Here the cooking is done, such as it is. Here they sit in the dark, or in such light as is supplied by the carefully-hoarded stock of fuel, till it is time to go to bed, and that is generally early enough. So rigid is the economy practised in many of these cottages that a candle is rarely, if ever, used."

[53] Henry Hunt, an astute observer, reporting on Wells labourers, in letters of November 1830, quoted one as saying "We dont want to do any mischief, but we want that poor children when they go to bed should have a belly full of 'tatoes instead of crying with half a belly full." At the end of November a letter to The Times said that 50 Melksham men were working for eight pence a day.

A teacher and some of the pupils of Miss Chinnock's private school,
with a donkey cart, at the rear of the school building, circa 1918.

A political demonstration at Church Street circa 1910. No.9, since re-built, was then a butcher's shop.

The Devizes, Melksham and Chippenham troops of mounted Yeomanry went into action against rioters at Oare, near Pewsey; at Stanton, Alton, Chirton and Horton and as the county faced a major breakdown of public order Market Lavington's bourgeoisie decided to try negotiation. A "meeting of Farmers," chaired by the respected local miller, Amram Saunders, met on 6 December, in response they said, to the urging of unnerved local magistrates to increase the pay of "the agricultural poor by as much as 25 per cent."

Details of the discussion have not survived, but we know enough of Amram's character and political beliefs - like his son he was a true 19th century radical - to expect it to have been heated. As his daughter, Anne, wrote at another time: "He did not, unfortunately, act in the affairs of the Parish or of the meeting house in the most conciliatory way. He made a great deal of turmoil at the parish meetings held in the vestry of the church. He liked to feel his neighbours' hearts beating with his own."

It is surprising, then, that this meeting produced a resolution, circulated in the press and on handbills sent to landowners, which was quite guarded and conciliatory and it is in stark contrast with another confrontation between the landed gentry and the village about half a century later which pulls no punches. It is important to remember, however, that in 1830 many of the "farmers" at the meeting were more often than not tenants of the big landowners like the Bouveries. The farmers were, in effect, responding to attempted buck-passing by the magistrates, who were either landowners themselves or were under pressure from landowners.

In any case the resolution is a fine example of avoidance of responsibility. It says that the tenant farmers had to pay high rents and tithes and were "totally disqualified" from paying labourers high wages or able to comply with the magistrates' demands "unless they be assisted by the proprietors of the land."[55] The farmers said that when they first rented the land they considered that a weekly pay to labourers should be the price of a bushel of wheat "and it is so regulated for many years." The recommendation of the magistrates would add a quarter to that price, the farmers claimed, so it was the landowners who should come to their assistance to make up the difference. The resolution goes on to say that "everyone should give employment to the poor" and the poor of Market Lavington should have small allotments of land to grow vegetables and where possible allotments of one acre or more should be let to "the industrious poor" at reasonable prices.

It concludes in ringing tones that "if all resolutions be carried into effect and every man in his respective station do his duty [shades of Nelson at Trafalgar] the poor man's state will be improved, and through the blessing of kind Providence, peace and order will be restored to our neighbourhood."[56]

It was not only the poor who were irritated and disillusioned by the tone of this appeal. The *Devizes Gazette* three days later carried an irate letter from "a Tenant" saying the landlords under attack should have been given time to consult with tenants about labourers' conditions. The letter went on to say that the meeting made it look as though "respectable tenants were disposed to range themselves openly on the side of the labouring class....."

The "labouring class" continued to protest and as violence occurred in more areas near Devizes the authorities over-reacted. The Yeomanry rode out with the Wiltshire Constabulary, plus "special constables," readily assisted by the ubiquitous informers. Only one informer is recorded in Market Lavington - William Merrett, a blacksmith, who claimed his reward for giving evidence against "and discovering" Gifford North, a Market Lavington labourer, who was apprehended in Dorset.

EMIGRANTS - FORCED AND OTHERWISE
North was one of the 300 people who appeared before a Special Commission at Salisbury that year and he was one of the 150 transported for seven years, 14 years, or life, to Australia. Many of those went to Tasmania, the hardest of penal colonies off the Australian mainland, but some, like North, were more fortunate and were assigned to New South Wales.

---

[54] As the protests grew in neighbouring counties the *Devizes and Wiltshire Gazette* devoted columns of its 11 November 1830 issue to a meeting in Calne deploring slavery and concomitant poverty in the West Indies. The irony would have been lost on all but a few readers like William Cobbett.

[55] William Cobbett saw the entire issue as one of over taxation and he wrote in the *Devizes Gazette* in October 1829 that "wretchedness is written on the face of every farmer in the country and the landowner himself, unless he have something besides his land, and dreads that he shall become little better than the paupers upon his estate."

[56] The Vicar of West Lavington was present at the meeting and he showed a constructive attitude by announcing later that he would reduce rents to tenants by 25 per cent. There were not many who followed his example, however.

[57] Of the 1,238 arrested, 32 were less than 18 years old, and 35 were more than 50. It was a young men's rising, largely because only the young and fit were able to work the long hours in the fields. The average age of the prisoners deported to New South Wales was 27 and half of them were married. In Australia the men were described by their gaolers as of a much better cast of character than the run-of-the-mill convict transported from Britain.

We know more about North than about any other villager before the end of the 19th century simply because of the thoroughness of the criminal justice records of the day. He was 25 at the time of his arrest,[57] and had married the year before to a Market Lavington woman four years his senior, Anne Luff or Love, daughter of James Luff and his wife Hannah, both of Market Lavington. Gifford North's first child, James, was born on 6 March 1831. At his trial Robert and Mary Pile gave evidence that he had "riotously assembled" at Alton Barnes and had broken into and demolished Pile's house and furniture. Pile also claimed that North had extorted a large sum of money from him by threats and violence, had wounded and beaten him, and had also broken up Pile's threshing machine.

The court sentenced North to death and commuted that sentence to transportation for life. Before being shipped to Australia, North was sent to the prison ship *The York* at Portsmouth and it was there recorded, presumably for future use in the colony of New South Wales, that his past career had taught him to "plough, reap, milk, sow." Also recorded were his physical characteristics: "five feet seven inches tall, ruddy complexion, brown hair, hazel eyes, small scar across back of left thumb, can read." He was assigned as a convict to the Clydesdale property in New South Wales where he obtained a conditional pardon in 1837. It seems that his wife, Ann, and son, James, did not leave England and the 1851 Census records Ann North, a widow, aged 50, living in Parsonage Lane with her son, John, an agricultural labourer, aged 28.

Mrs North chose to call herself a widow, but she may have divorced North. In any case two more marriages lay ahead of him in Australia. By the first of these he had another son Gifford, born in 1847 in Windsor, west of Sydney, at which time he described himself as a farmer. His third wife, Maria Gardner, gave him two more children, both daughters, born in 1853 and 1854. At the time of Gifford North senior's death from "the effects of intemperance" in Windsor in 1866, after 36 years in New South Wales, he is listed as having only two teenage daughters.

It would be encouraging to report that after the riots which sent Gifford North on his long, rough road to the other side of the world there was a sharp improvement in the lot of the agricultural workers. There was not and as early as 1831 the Yeomanry were called out to disperse riots in Ramsbury and later in the year there was an agricultural labourers' strike in West Lavington which failed to force employers to increase wages. In Market Lavington, in 1833, the parish decided that all labourers without work should go to the Market Place from 6 a.m. to 7 a.m. and from noon to 1 p.m. daily to check whether there were jobs available. Whether the workers did so and for how long is unclear.

By 1834 the *Devizes and Wiltshire Gazette* - then the mouthpiece of privilege and complacency - was deploring "the moral deterioration" of men in Wroughton who were demonstrating against the indifference of their employers to the conditions of the workhouse. Their demonstration, if it can be so dignified, consisted of smoking in the cemetery and clearly this would do nothing to convince those whose profits were threatened that there should be any real increase in wages. In fact, by 1844, the average wage was still seven shillings and in 1850, one Wiltshire village, South Damerham, had the lowest rate - six shillings - in England. By the middle of the century bands of men, sometimes 200-strong, went from farm to farm in the Wiltshire valleys seeking a nine shillings a week wage and it was not until later in the century that a ten shilling a week wage was the average.

For single men one solution was to marry early because married men usually had a better chance of finding and keeping jobs, so in Wiltshire in the mid-19th century the average marrying age for men was 18 and for girls 15 or 16. Many families saved what they could and emigrated to the colonies. In 1830 a William Tanner, of Lockridge, persuaded 50 farmworkers to emigrate to Australia, and a large party of workers from Lacock went to Canada in 1832. The parishes also saw emigration of the poor as a way of reducing the cost of maintaining them in the poor-houses. Market Lavington parish officers noted in January 1845 that a pauper, John Philpott, who was resident in the Union Workhouse, wished to emigrate to North America and it agreed that it should pay the handsome sum of £15 13s. 6d. to permit him to do so.[58] Philpott must have been a serious nuisance or a most deserving case because in 1849 the churchwardens resolved to raise the sum of £8 towards the expenses of all paupers who were willing to emigrate.

Two of these emigrants were from the Market Lavington area: Alfred Saunders, the son of Amram (see page 73), and a young carpenter from Market Lavington, James Draper. Anne Saunders says in her book *Russell Mill* that Alfred resolved to emigrate to New Zealand because he and his father were incompatible. He prospered in the new colony and became a member of the New Zealand Parliament's Legislative Assembly. Presumably Draper was looking for another world. They sailed in *The Fifeshire*, for Nelson, New Zealand, and on board they and others formed a Temperance Society which Alfred imported into Nelson and, according to Anne "did very much to form the character of the new colony." James kept a journal during his voyage and Anne provides us with two extracts:

"Sunday, 20 October 1841. We came in sight of

---

[58] About a hundred years later the British Government was asking prospective emigrants to Australia to pay only £10 for their passage.

land this morning, being the island of Madeira. We had Divine service performed today, by the doctor, for the first time. I felt greatly pleased; it reminded me of the last time being at the Market Lavington church, hearing the same prayers. I am this afternoon with Mr Saunders and Mr Cotterell, practising some sacred tunes, in order to meet this evening with the other gentlemen to have Divine service performed, which I expect I shall much enjoy. Books have been distributed today amongst the emigrants. This is the happiest day I have spent here yet. I enjoyed myself much this evening. We sang three times, I accompanying the same with my flute."

The second entry, in November, reads: "About two o'clock one of our young men called me, in haste, on deck. I immediately went up. It was to see the porpoise fish by many hundreds, I may say thousands, jumping and playing. It was the most amusing and pleasing sight I have yet witnessed. Thermometer stands at 82."

It was among the last of James's diary entries. He complained of feeling ill and one day Alfred found him in his cabin with tears on his cheeks. Alfred sat by his side for six days and five nights but on the evening of 26 November he died, and at noon the following day was buried at sea.

James Draper had learned a trade which could have supported him at home, but in the 1840's one in seven men in Wiltshire were agricultural workers and this was a precarious life, remaining so for another three-quarters of a century. By 1930 one in 14 was working on the land and in 1960 the figure was one in 20. Man and horse had given way to the machine.

One early machine, a travelling thresher, was invented by a Mr Cambridge of Market Lavington as early as the 1840's and though successful it did not attract the hostile attention of the agrarian labourers of the parish as had the threshing machine of Robert Pile, North's victim, during the uprising.

EDUCATION

In the earlier history of Market Lavington education was for the sons and daughters of families who could afford to keep their children out of the work-force. St Mary's Church began a Sunday School, in 1790, which taught other subjects than religion. One of the first purchases by the school was a hundred copies of a booklet entitled *Reading Made Easy*.

A trade directory of 1791-1798 refers to "a charity school for 36 children who have books given them, and the girls are taught to knit and sow," but it is unclear what happened in later years to this classic example of sexism in the schoolroom. The first formal schooling in Market Lavington was one set up in 1802 for paying day-boys. A few non-paying boys joined classes in 1818. By 1833 there were four day schools in East Lavington and one in Easterton.

Two sisters, the daughters of Amram Saunders,

opened a school at Lavington, in Parsonage Lane, at the Parsonage House. Elizabeth Saunders, the moving force in this venture "had immense decision and determination of character and was anything but a lamb," according to her neice, Anne, writing in her book on Lavington, *Russell Mill*. The Saunders sisters, especially Elizabeth, were "greatly stirred by the preaching of the new preachers," and it is clear that much of their school curriculum reflected this preaching and Elizabeth told Anne that she was "determined to withstand the corruption of the place." [Market Lavington].

The Parsonage House pupils learned other skills than avoiding the temptations of village life, however. Anne Saunders says "Girls learnt to do plain needlework very nicely, and with great facility, also learned dancing and a few other things. But the range of their pursuits was not wide; it was supposed then that children must have time to grow and could not be doing everything. Those things were selected which were likely to be most useful to girls of small fortune, and at home they received good instruction from their parents in a variety of household work."

In 1844 the Radnor family gave land adjoining the churchyard for a public school which opened its doors the next year. It cost £620 and voluntary contribution raised the money. In 1859 the school had about a hundred male and female pupils. The teachers had no formal qualifications and the girls' classes were considered unsatisfactory. This may have been a so-called British School.

These schools were the creation of Joseph Lancaster, a Quaker, who founded the British and Foreign School Society in 1810, and by 1851 there were 1,500 individual British Schools nationally. Their chief attraction was that they were cheap to run as partially-educated children took classes in the place of qualified teachers and they were paid only a small wage.

A so-called National School came later. In addition, Harriet Tucker ran a boarding school in the village; schools for young ladies were opened in 1879 and 1899; and about 30 children from non-conformist families were taught in private houses. In 1865 Louisa Hay of Clyffe Hall offered £1,000 to build either a school or a church at Easterton and as a compromise a building which could serve as both was built and opened in 1867. Mrs Hay paid the salary of the mistress. Classes were free.

Separate state schools for girls and boys opened in 1863 and these were not amalgamated until 1914. A problem for all schools, not just in Market Lavington but in all rural areas of the county, was attendance. In 1876, for instance, only 64.5 per cent of the children were at school during the months when their parents needed help in picking potatoes and peas. After 1880 school authorities obtained the power to enforce attendance, but even then children living two miles from the school were out of reach of the new bylaws.

A teacher at the boys' school from 1879 to 1892, Mr Hatley[59] (and later his successors), kept a log recording attendance, punishments, and other significant events. Hatley writes that the great storm of 1881 brought three foot drifts in the school-yard and there were no lessons for several days. In late September 1891, only 29 boys out of 53 registered were at school, because the harvest was near completion. Another entry, in 1897, says that "gentlemen" were illegally employing about 14 boys every week as beaters in the shooting season. The teacher comments that "this is the kind of thing I have to contend with during the autumn. Some of the boys have not even passed Standard 3."

Hatley, like all teachers of his time and later, used the cane liberally. He records that Herbert Cooper was "soundly thrashed for doing wilful damage to a tombstone in the churchyard. His mother came to school in the afternoon in a furious state to demand an explanation, as, according to her, he had expiated his fault by paying two shillings and sixpence towards 30 shillings worth of damage. As it was at Mr [Walter] Bouverie's request the boy was thrashed, Mrs Cooper piously expressed her determination to give that gentleman a piece of her mind. Happily the broad Atlantic, I believe rolls between her and the object of her wrath." [Bouverie was in America].

The most heartfelt entry is Hatley's last: "Having become thoroughly convinced of the futility of one teacher attempting to teach 60 boys in seven standards, and in at least seven separate subjects (reading, writing, arithmetic, geog., English, drawing and Scripture) I have recently sent in my resignation. The difficulty is vastly increased by the wretched attendance which has prevailed throughout the year..... Have asked to be allowed to go at Christmas."

The girls also had a log of events and this too notes poor attendance. In August during the first year of the school opening, 1863, the teacher notes that four girls "went home at eleven to cook dinners for their parents who were out reaping."

The joint school of more than a hundred pupils felt the impact of two world wars. In 1915 a female teacher left to do Red Cross duty and in 1916 the head teacher was called up. In 1940 there was an influx of evacuee children from Greater London and the staff issued gas masks. The school survived another 31 years before closing at the end of the spring term 1971.

---

[59] The children recited this rhyme about him:
"Daddy Hatley is a good man,
He tries to teach us all he can,
Reading, writing, and arithmetic,
And he doesn't forget his great big stick."

GHOSTS AND SPELLS

Market Lavington has at least three documented ghosts. Parsonage House in Parsonage Lane, replaced in the 1860's by two cottages, supposedly was haunted by a lady who had been murdered, leaving her blood on the floorboards. The best account of her presence is from November 1818, when, says the witness, 57 years after the event: "I went up to my room - it was the one with the marks of blood on the floor. Some time after I distinctly saw a white figure glide into the room; it went around by the wash-stand by the bed, and there disappeared. I fainted." Another witness, who recalled a time when the Parsonage had been a school, said that once, when the children were assembled, they heard "a terrible noise, just as if buckets of lime were being emptied from a height on to the floor below us." The vicar offered to search the place and found nothing.

The second ghost has an inferior pedigree though reportedly it was seen by people over many years on the Market Lavington to Easterton road, at Lattice Bridge, below Fiddington House. Supposedly, when an ancient hedge was replaced by a wall in the early 20th century, three skeletons were found. They were re-buried in Market Lavington churchyard and, so the report says, the ghost, or ghosts, are now at rest.

The third comes from a reliable witness, who was staying in a house in the High Street when she encountered a strange little old man sitting in the corner of a newly refurbished bedroom. She chose not to spend the night in the room for understandable reasons. The family forgot the story until many years later they learned from an elderly resident that in his childhood a strange little old man had indeed spent time in a much earlier version of the house.

A fourth apparition with overtones of farce is said to be that of the ever-dignified 19th century squire, Edward Pleydell Bouverie, running through the woods of the Manor at the time of its sale in 1914.

There are also, however, occasional allegedly documented happenings, which might be described as paranormal. There are the great trees on the edge of the woods of Dauntsey Manor, under which, says legend, there are buried restless ill-doers, and these trees are said to move occasionally. Among other large moving objects is the "drill barn" in Parsonage Lane which "shifted" three inches east one night in 1987 - in a paranormal near-hurricane.

The spells and cures, and potions handed down in Market Lavington's excellent Women's Institute scrapbooks, though nearly 150 years old, may not be exclusive to Market Lavington. Perhaps other Wiltshire villagers rub their eyes with a gold ring to cure sties. An alternative offered is putting the afflicted eye to a keyhole facing the east wind. Not precisely a potion, but worth a try for those with time on their hands, is a shampoo made from borax "the size of a nut," a large handful of rosemary picked from the stalk, and one "knotted marjoram," all put in a stone jar, to which boiling rainwater is added. This must then be left standing "on the hob" for three days, then strained through muslin; the brew to be strengthened by two pence worth of camphor, two pence worth of glycerine and a wine glass of rum. Also on offer is a recipe for nine gallons of ginger wine.

ROADS AND TRANSPORT

From the earliest times even remote villages were linked to the outside world by tracks, and for many centuries these tracks have remained virtually as they were without change. The premier prehistoric trackway of southern England was the Ridgeway, but there must have been many others now lost. The Romans, the greatest road builders of the ancient world, saw roads in strategic military terms and in the wake of the legions came the Saxons, who used the Roman roads but built their own trackways in the vales and river valleys below Salisbury Plain, in the places which the Romans had ignored. There were Saxon roads from Burbage to Pewsey, and south along the Avon valley to Amesbury and Old Salisbury, as well as along the south bank of the Wylye and the north bank of the Nadder. White Street, in Market Lavington, led to the ancient way across the Plain, and Main Street was part of an ancient track which led from the vale of Pewsey to Edington, Westbury, Warminster, and the south-west.

The Saxon and Norman travellers sought but not always found security on their roads. By the 11th century there were four main roads or "Streets" which boasted that they enjoyed what was referred to as the King's special peace. In the area of Wiltshire there was the Fosse Way from Bath to Cirencester, and Ermine Street, through the centre of the county.

Elsewhere, not only security but the condition of the tracks were a constant worry for regular travellers and we find that as early as the 13th century well-to-do merchants were farsighted enough to leave money in their wills for the improvement of roads over which their descendants would travel. The condition of the roads, if that is not too grand a word, is hard to appreciate today. Some idea of them may be gained by those well enough shod, who, after wet weather, venture onto tracks leading from the Plain to Market Lavington village. Driving laden wagons over the foot-deep mud of the main thoroughfares of even a century ago must have been heart-stopping labour.

The dominant fact of life in road travel for more than 70 years were the turnpikes. The roads in the neighbourhood of Market Lavington were controlled by

11 turnpikes, and covered 21 miles, following the Turnpike Act of 1752, but they were bitterly resented. The turnpikes had come into being simply because there was no effective highway authority and, absurdly, the parish and not the county was charged with the upkeep of highroads. The parishes were not able to meet the challenge and parliament granted private companies, in the form of Turnpike Trusts, to erect gates and toll bars and, in effect, tax the road users in return for maintaining the highway. There is no doubt that travel by road improved as a result and by 1840 there were 22,000 miles of good turnpike roads in England, with nearly 8,000 toll gates and side bars.

By that time, however, Market Lavington and its neighbours had literally burned their toll-gates. The 11 turnpike gates built in the area by the local squirarchy in the mid-18th century, had later been let to interested entrepreneurs for about £450 a year and it was a good investment as the renters were earning up to £700 a year in collections at the turnpike. That was not all profit, however, as theoretically the money was to be used for road repairs and payment of the toll-keeper, who usually lived in a nearby cottage, spending part of his day in a toll-booth.

One of Market Lavington's 11 toll-gates was approaching the steep section of the road to the West Lavington cross-roads. Another was on Kings Road, now a minor road signposted to Easterton Sands, and a third was on the Lavington-Urchfont Road. Charges were levelled according to the type of traffic. A six-horse carriage paid one shilling and sixpence to pass through a gate, a four-horse carriage a shilling, and those drawn by fewer than four horses sixpence. Horses alone cost a penny, cattle ten pence per score, and sheep, dogs, calves and other animals five pence per score. Church-goers, funerals, post-carriages, soldiers and Devizes people "taking the air," provided they returned through the gate within two hours, were free.

In August 1824 villagers north of the Plain raised £2,051 by voluntary subscription to buy out the lessees. Contributors included Captain (later Admiral) Duncombe Playdell Bouverie, Messrs. Amram Saunders and Fowle (who contributed £100 each) while others included Messrs. Gauntlett, Smith and Stagg. On a chill early February night in 1825 a party of men from Market Lavington and Littleton Pannell, led by Saunders, raided the toll-gates, took them off their hinges and paraded with them through the streets before carrying them up White Street and onto the Plain for a bonfire.

On the night of 8 February the formal celebration of the end of the tolls was held at the Green Dragon, with the "president" pro-tem, Duncombe Playdell Bouverie in the chair. The healths of the prime movers in the disposal of the gates, Messrs. Saunders,[60] Box and Tinker were drunk repeatedly, with some 20 further toasts thereafter and songs written for the occasion were rendered by "the composers." On the Plain above, an immense bonfire, sky-rockets and the firing of four cannons, "the property of neighbouring gentlemen," startled the neighbourhood. Commenting on the dinner one press item said: "As one looks at the toast list one wonders if the following morning was quite so happy and joyous, but perhaps the heads of those days were stronger than ours today." The dinner was repeated on 8 February for many years. The villagers celebrated the following night with another bonfire in the Market Place, around which the inhabitants danced, after being given "a moderate portion of strong beer." Market Lavington and its neighbours had every reason to feel proud of their achievement. The Devizes Turnpike Trust was not abolished until 1868.

Because the turnpikes had kept the roads in order for three quarters of a century, the public had come to expect to travel any distance by road, and road surfaces and coach travel had improved greatly. Wagons drawn by four great horses, their bells ringing to make way for them, superseded the pack-horse and Tantivy coaches travelled up to ten miles an hour for hundreds of miles, using relays of horses at the coaching inns. Before 1840 a coach from Salisbury to Chippenham passed through West Lavington every alternate day, and Market Lavington was well-served by the wagoners.

In 1841 a carrier of goods went from the Green Dragon to Hungerford Station via Pewsey for the London train on Mondays, Wednesdays and Fridays. Another carrier hauled goods to Bath from houses in the village every Tuesday morning and on Saturdays he went to Trowbridge. Another went to Devizes from his house on Mondays and Thursdays, and an Easterton carrier went to Devizes via Market Lavington daily.

Passenger travel over long distances by horse-drawn coach was partly superseded by the railways at the end of the 19th century, but there was competition still from the horse-drawn short-distance coaches and hauliers. Occasionally the local hauliers provided a long-distance outing to London. The one which was to provide villagers with their first sight of the Great Exhibition of 1851 proved something of a fiasco, however, as a number of the party spent the day at the Wagon and Horses inn at Paddington.

A Market Lavington-born man, Edwin Potter began a horse-drawn bus service running from Market Lavington to Devizes in 1872, and later he built a bus drawn by two horses, to carry 14 passengers, with blue and white matching wheels and a black weather-proof

---

[60] Villagers presented Saunders with a silver service for his efforts. Saunders, like his son, Samuel, was a difficult man, at least according to his daughter Anne. At one point she speaks of a friend being "a lively, humorous, chivalrous gentleman..... a very different man from my father."

Men working on the construction of the Great Western main rail line through the Parham Wood area.
In the background are the remains of a farmhouse and buildings which were demolished.
The last occupant of the farm was a Mr John Sainsbury.

The 'Motor Bus'. In 1911 Mr Fred Sayers started his 'bus company in the Market Place.
Here he is, at the wheel, en route to Devizes.

hood. It was not a comfortable trip because the heavy iron wheels amplified every rut in the road, but Potter boasted that he would get the mail and parcels through in all weather from Easterton to Lavington, through Littleton Panell and Potterne to Devizes. His 9.30 a.m. coach to Devizes Post Office caught the 11.00 mail train from Devizes to Bristol most days and he ran two buses on market days. For the occasional house-removal he used a 12-horse dray and this service continued until 1916 when the larger motor-vehicle made it uncompetitive. Potter died in 1921, aged 89.

His service's successor was the Lavington and Devizes Motor Service run and owned by Fred Sayers. Eventually Mr Sayers had 37 vehicles - mostly the "Crossley tenders" which were popular with the Royal Flying Corps and later the R.A.F. He adapted them into charabancs when the day-trip craze began in the 1920's. By 1924 he had covered buses, seating 14 or 32, for special tours, and operated a daily Lavington to Devizes service, for two shillings return, which was later extended to Bath, via Seend, Melksham, Atworth and Box for three shillings return. There was an earlier firm of carriers which ran vans from the Green Dragon inn every Thursday, through Pewsey, Hungerford, Newbury, Reading and Maidenhead to London, and the same firm went to Frome from the Green Dragon every Tuesday.

The construction of the Stert-Westbury rail line began in April 1897 and took three years to complete. At times a thousand men were at work and because the contractors were well-behind schedule they offered workers fivepence-halfpenny an hour. The station at Littleton Panell was known as Lavington Station. The station hotel building survives.

LATER BOUVERIES

The second Lord Radnor, who acquired Market Lavington from the Abingdon estates, willed his holdings to his second son, Duncombe Pleydell Bouverie (he of anti-turnpike fame, see page 78). Duncombe retired from the navy and entered politics, winning a House of Commons seat for Salisbury in the elections of 1828 and 1830. In his pre-election manifesto, in 1832, he spoke of his "humble exertion in the House of Commons for procuring a full and free representation of the people." He supported the extension of suffrage to the householder who paid ten pounds or more annual rates, who Bouverie said he found "intelligent, independent and activated by public spirit of the most disinterested kind."

He retired from politics in 1835. His country home was Clyffe Hall from 1812 until his death in 1850, when the entire estate, including the Old House, returned to William, third Earl of Radnor (1779-1869), though Duncombe Pleydell Bouverie's only daughter, Louisa, widow of the Honourable Samuel Hay (died 1847) continued to live at Clyffe Hall until her death in 1898.

In an era of limited tolerance, William, the third Earl, as a member of the House of Lords, actively opposed corporal punishment in the army, the excessive use of ex-officio information against the press and, in general, his aim was to promote social reform. Market Lavington residents of the time (1845) would have appreciated William's protests against the Allotment Bill; legislation which he said would strike at the independence of agricultural labourers and have a tendency to lower wages at a time when wages were at bedrock. He was a close friend and active supporter of William Cobbett and it was said that he was the only man with whom Cobbett never quarrelled.

William left the Market Lavington portion of his inheritance to his second son, Edward (1818-1889), a man of quite different mould and views. Edward was educated at Harrow and Trinity College, Cambridge, and was called to the bar in 1843. He soon entered parliament as Liberal M.P. for Kilmarnock, Scotland, though his background lay in Wiltshire. By the age of 54 he was described by *Vanity Fair* as one of "that elder and steadier school of Liberal politicians," associated with Lord Palmerston. That was his public, political face. Some of those closer to him often found him inclined to pomposity and arrogance.

He was also a male chauvinist, even, apparently, among the males of his time, and a descendant, Anthony Wilson, who has reacted against a chauvinist family tradition, has written a book called *The Female Pest, An Expose Of Misogynist Mythology*. In a separate article, Wilson notes that one relative, repelled by Edward's attitude to women, hung Edward's portrait below that of his wife. In a speech to the Commons in 1871 Edward quoted the Bible to remind his fellow parliamentarians that a wife's "desire shall be to her husband and he shall rule over her," and he was quick to oppose female suffrage. He also voted for the retention of flogging in the army - in contrast with his father's views on the issue (see above).

Edward appears also to have had grandiose ideas which, on occasion, verged on the eccentric. Thus he would not eat from the railway's first class china when he travelled by train, but brought with him his own 'train set' of white china with E.P.B. engraved on it in gold.

He inherited a valuable but not large estate of about 1,800 acres at Market Lavington, but lived at Coleshill House, Highworth, in Buckinghamshire while architects and builders put into effect his plans for a Victorian Gothic manor house on the outskirts of Market Lavington village. Building and landscaping, including the cutting down of woodland to obtain a view of three churches, began in 1862 and lasted seven years. Later the new "lord" of the manor authorised the destruction of several small farm-houses as part of his woodland landscaping. The so-called Market Lavington Manor, completed in 1869 at a cost of £67,000 (at least £4,500,000 at today's prices) was really Victorian kitsch

The Co-operative Stores in the High Street, circa 1927.

Church Street. The photo was taken from opposite the Vicarage. Before the Hopkins occupied No.21 the Price family ran a horsedrawn coach service from the premises. Three cottages on the right were demolished and the site is now the front garden of Church Cottage. The lime trees on the right are in front of Nos.18 and 20.

The Box family in front of their home on the site of the Brickworks which they owned and ran during the greater part of the 19th century. The house is now known as Mowbray House.

with its ill-assorted borrowing from earlier architectural periods. When Edward and his wife moved in there were 24 bedrooms, an hydraulic lift for moving coals and luggage to higher floors, and light from gas-lamps on the ground-floor. There was also stabling for 12 horses, and bedrooms for coachmen and grooms above a coach house. William Box, of Market Lavington, supplied the bricks. It must have been his largest order by far.

There are suggestions that the house's interior decoration reflected Masonic principles and certainly the fifth and sixth Earls Radnor were very prominent in Free Masonry. Clearly the manor was a statement in stone of a wealthy younger son who was determined to assert his right to be considered a man of property and power. The house is now part of Dauntsey's School.

In politics Edward's aspirations were of the highest. He sought to be Speaker of the Commons, followed by the inevitable peerage, but this was denied him, perhaps unfairly. He certainly did not lack courage. He bitterly opposed his own party leader and Prime Minister, Gladstone, over Irish issues and other measures. In one felicitous turn of phrase he told the Commons that he "regretted that the Prime Minister should amuse his leisure hours by driving a coach and six through Acts of Parliament," and when the Liberal ministry was defeated he failed to be re-elected in the election of 1874. He retired from politics and entered the markets but unfortunately for him - and for Market Lavington - his departure from the national scene coincided with the agricultural depression caused, in part, by cheap imports from abroad.

The fortunes of the Lavington Bouveries went into a decline, never to recover. Misjudgements there were and financial commitments left the estate over-extended, and as the years passed the depression deepened. In 1888, the year before Edward's death, he intervened to bail out a tenant and, in doing so, saddled the estate with a non-profit-making enterprise. The property, of more than 2,000 acres, was his, and he had leased it out to Richard Sargent, one of four brothers all of whom were heavily in debt with no prospect of being able to meet their creditors.

The creditors (including James Gye of Market Lavington) met in Devizes in late January and expressed their fears that as the Sargents were leaving the estates they would have to try to run them themselves. Sargent owed Pleydell Bouverie £18,000 in back rent (in fact his liabilities were more than £30,000 and his cash in hand was £211) and at the Devizes hearing Bouverie told the creditors that when it became apparent some years before that Sargent was unable to meet his payments on time he had agreed to reduce them provisionally, but this had not helped matters. Now he announced he would buy Sargent's stock, farm-house, barns and tillage, in settlement of the debt. The creditors were relieved, but Edward had shouldered one more burden.

VILLAGE LIFE

For reasons which will become apparent this is the moment when we should look at the village community of the 19th century and remind ourselves that Market Lavington is fortunate in having a fine museum which is bringing together a visual record of its history in this period. Thousands of old photographs, artefacts and memorabilia, for the most part record high days and holidays, but behind them there is a story covering centuries of slow growth and change. Though anecdotes can capture some moments, before the invention of photography there was little other than the registers of baptisms, marriages and burials, plus bricks and mortar -including gravestones - preserving the passing of the years.

It is fascinating to examine the ancient festivals and ways of life which downland villages and towns like Market Lavington preserved long after they had faded from memory in the more urbanised areas. Centuries ago the village was renowned for its "church ales," once sponsored by all the parishes on the anniversaries of the founding of their churches. Market Lavington retained the custom long after other villages had abandoned it.

A description of the village taken from *Pigot's Directory 1830* is interesting: "The houses which are tolerably well built are ranged in two streets, through one of which passes the high road from Devizes to Shrewton. The malting business is extensively carried on here, and there are some good houses of public entertainment for the accommodation of travellers; of these the Green Dragon and Wheel inns merit particular mention. The Earl of Radnor is lord of the manor, and holds a court baron twice a year. The market is a very large one for corn and cattle and is held on Wednesday. The annual fair is held on 10 August. The Parish has 1,438 inhabitants."

At that time Market Lavington was a place of traditions - good and bad but mainly bad, according to some revivalist preachers and puritans of the late 18th century. Here is one description which was preserved by Amram Saunders' daughter, Anne Saunders (1819-1903):

"A common ruin of all that is holy seems to have pervaded society from the highest to the lowest; nor did the condition appear to awaken any concern. Bull and badger baiting, cock and dog fighting, with all their concomitant evils and depravity of manners, pugilistic encounters, drunkenness, and profanity were the characteristics of the people. Such were the people of Lavington, not only of the lower, but also of the middle and upper classes, and these things were not only sanctioned but encouraged by the clergy. To such an extent did this run that the place was notorious for wickedness for miles round. In the Establishment the teaching was a meagre maudling something, for neither in precept nor example could it be called religion, not even morality. It was such teaching as might be expected where the sports of the field, the facilities for angling, and the pleasures of good fellowship were objects of pre-eminent attraction to clerical ambition."

"The submission of the poor to their superiors; reverence and obedience to the commands of the priesthood; abject veneration for the Established Church; punctuality in attendance on her rites and ceremonies, with a full and prompt discharge of all her dues. These were the staple of her instructions, and all that was required by her to constitute a good man and a Christian, or to entitle him to heaven. Every effort made to instruct and enlighten the mind received the whole weight of her opposition and anathema, as it was considered far preferable that the population be left in the grossest darkness, perfectly and profoundly ignorant of the claims of God."

"So besotted in vice were they, that to be the best fighter, to have the best bull-dog, to possess the finest game bird, or to have won the prize in any of those sports was the highest felicity and enjoyment their minds could desire or appreciate."[61]

Anne Saunders does not name the writer of this letter, but he was a certain John Foster who penned it after a visit to the village in 1790. She appeared to have agreed whole-heartedly with his evaluation of the village she knew some half-century later when she adds that her great-uncle James Garrett - "a pleasant, clever, gentlemanly man of a very unscrupulous moral character..... delighted especially in making merry on the Sabbath-day" and the Sabbath eve was "actually at one time in that valley devoted to revelry and drunkenness."

She goes on to mention that the wife of her great-uncle's brother, Captain John Garrett "made the discovery that she was not the sole possessor of his affections but that he was quite as good-natured to some other lady." As a result she hanged herself and Anne Saunders says "Such were my father's predecessors! Such was Lavington! Such were the men of Lavington!" Anne adds that there were, however, preachers who tried to help Lavington mend its ways, including one from Imber, "an orator in a rough way," who mounted a large stone in the Market Place and preached. Another, a Mr Sloper of Devizes, also preached "although he went in and out of the place almost at the risk of his life."

There is without doubt exaggeration by the otherwise unknown Foster and by a prim Victorian lady here, but we do know that Market Lavington, like Potterne, had long been known as a village which went its own way. People worked hard and played hard. The social activities which are mentioned by Anne

Saunders' anonymous critic were widespread in the English countryside at one time. His or her horror may stem from the fact that they had faded already in the cities and bigger towns of other counties with which he was familiar.

Wiltshire itself held to a rugged, older life-style well into the 18th century. The summer Quarter Sessions in Devizes were held at 7 a.m., farmworkers rose at 4.30 a.m., and men, women, and children took their dinner before noon and went to bed with the dying of the light. Candles were a luxury in many homes in Market Lavington as late as the 18th century and even the comparatively well-to-do town tradesmen thought twice before lighting a fire in the house except in the depth of winter. Fuel was often in short supply and theft of it was common. Into the 20th century neither lord nor villager had the habit of bathing and one of the then more prestigious houses in the village, the Old House, did not have a bathroom until 1939, half a century after a niece of the third Earl of Radnor had moved in.

An ancient and often abused official method of differentiating one villager from another revolved around ownership of property and this provided the rate-paying property-owner with voting rights which were denied to tenants, and Market Lavington's electoral rolls for the early part of the last century make scandalous reading. In 1818, for instance, when the population of Market Lavington must have exceeded a thousand, just 28 men[62] were eligible to vote and a few of those 28 did not live in the village or even in the county. The reason was that most of the dwellings in the village were owned by the Radnor estate or by absentee landlords. The Reform Act of 1832 aimed to correct this disenfranchisement but in the election two years later only 25 Market Lavingtonians had their say about who should represent them in the Commons. Among them was John Ward of Devizes, who is listed as owning a freehold house, shop and garden occupied by Robert Dowse and others. Dowse "and others" had no vote. By 1839 the number of registered property owner-voters had risen to only 55 and it was not until the Reform Act of 1867 that the village, the county and the nation could be said to be electing a representative government. With the 1867 legislation all male occupiers of dwelling houses who had resided in the property for 12 months and who had been rated to pay rates as occupiers and, equally importantly, all lodgers who had occupied lodgings for 12 months to the annual value, unfurnished, of £10, became entitled to vote.

Inevitably the broader franchise eroded the distinction between the haves and the have-nots in the

---

[61] From Anne Saunders' book *Russell Mill*, in a chapter headed "Benighted Lavington." Unfortunately she does not reveal the source for these fire and brimstone opinions. One must remember, however, that she was a staunch Chapel-goer and was less than worldly in some respects.

[62] Female suffrage was a hundred years in the future.

village, but through the centuries Market Lavington does not appear to have suffered unduly from class divisions. Its ancient origins as a weavers' town onto which opportunistic "foreign" landowners grafted their grandiose constructions, put something of a check on the class divisions more obvious in some neighbouring villages. There was, however, a hierarchy which took hold in the 18th century and blossomed in the 19th at least until economic depression and world war swept the old order away.

So, the word "manor" evoked power and privilege in villages like Market Lavington long after it had lost its significance in the world outside. The fact was that while manorial titles had been bought or earned from the monarch for a thousand years, by Queen Victoria's time there was often no monarchical sanction for such titles and anyone who had the price of the land and someone else's ancestral home could design his shield, write his motto and become the local "lord."

There was a 19th century lord of the manor of Market Lavington simply because Edward Pleydell Bouverie had received a present of it from his father. That present was his stepping stone to influence at county and national level, provided he was mentally agile and a hundred years earlier there could not have been any of the questioning of his stewardship which was to come.

Next most important in the village hierarchy were the lord's relatives, if resident in the village. For most of the last third of the 19th century these were Louisa Hay at Clyffe Hall, and Edward's unmarried son and daughter, who were usually more accessible. Next in line came the Vicar, followed by gentlemen of leisure (Market Lavington was usually too down-to-earth to harbour many of those), then the manorial agent, followed by the village and church officers, the trades people, and in turn the Bouverie employees, the coachmen, grooms and household servants - the people "in service" and beneath all came the agrarian labourers with or without their overseers.

Three vignettes, two from the 19th century and the other from the 20th capture the changing relationship between powers, great and small, and the village folk. Fear and respect of the hierarchy in Queen Victoria's reign is the essence of the story of a farm lad who was out with his gun on the Bouverie estate when he accidentally shot the game-keeper's dog. He ran home and asked a village elder what he should do. "Join the army," was the response. (He did, saw the world and lived to be 80, not regretting the course he had taken.)

The second story comes from the Devizes Quarter sessions in 1834, when an overseer on a road repair near Market Lavington had one of the village labourers brought into court for threatening him. In evidence it emerged that the overseer had told the man that he was deducting seven pence from his daily wage of eight pence because the overseer had found out that the man's wife was earning seven pence a day from her own work. The judge ruled in the labourer's favour but the point of the story is that the case reached court only because the overseer had gone ridiculously too far. Overseers were lords of their little patch.

The third story comes from the first third of the 20th century and concerns the Warrington family, who had bought Clyffe Hall. After their arrival at the Hall and before their first attendance at Sunday service in St Mary's it was suggested to the churchwardens that those villagers then occupying the front pew in the church should vacate it in deference to the newly arrived Lord and Lady. The villagers refused. The additional anecdote about Lady Warrington is that she asked a churchwarden to tell one of the teenage village girls to change the shoes she wore to church because their soles were too noisy. The message was passed on and the girl wrote a letter to milady telling her that she had no intention of changing her shoes or their soles.

The 19th century was a time not only for "knowing one's place" but also for aspiring to something above that place. The trend was towards "gentrification" or what today we call upward mobility, visible in the trade directories which doubled as roll calls of who was anybody in the countryside from a trader to a gentleman. The 1841 directory listed eight of these self-styled gentlemen, one of whom was Admiral Duncombe Pleydell Bouverie, an earlier owner of Clyffe Hall; and among the others was the vicar.

One Market Lavington tradesman was content to be known by his trade in the 1830 directory, but he chose to be known as a member of "the gentry and clergy" of the village in a directory of 1842. The tithe roll for 1840 shows who owned the larger tracts of land. First, of course, was the third Earl Radnor, who owned 1,247 acres, then Duncombe Pleydell Bouverie, with 550; Henry and Elizabeth Legg with 44; John Hayward, with 430; and Robert Langford with 110. Among "occupiers" were Thomas Fowle, renting 1351 acres; Robert French, 609; Henry Philpot, 152; and Richard Box with 106.

Trade directories like Pigot and Co.'s, Slaters and Gregory's showed a thriving trading community in the village 150 years ago. The reason is, of course, that a community of 1,115 in 1841 did its shopping in the village High Street and not in towns five or 30 miles away. What public transport there was, was slow and infrequent so Market Lavington's 57 tradesmen made a living from villagers.

There was a quite remarkable number of trades people who the village supported. Some of these retailers passed on their skills within the family. There were Dowses who were butchers in Market Lavington more than two hundred years ago. And Market Lavington, until recent times had a tobacconist and had one as early as 1637, when John Hope paid the very large sum of £5 a year for his license to sell a product which had been known to Britain for only 72 years.

Norman Neate, the last brewer in the village, accompanied by two Canadian soldiers at the rear of the Brewery Tap (now Nos.7 & 9 White Street) during the First World War.

The traders included five bootmakers, four tailors, three straw-bonnet makers, three butchers, three wheelwrights, three blacksmiths, three corn dealers and four maltsters, plus nine grocers, three of whom also listed themselves as drapers. Interestingly, there was only one miller, Amram Saunders; and one lodging house, run by Elizabeth Halfpenny; but Ezra Price offered himself as a pianoforte tuner, and Walter Tucker had two hats - as auctioneer/appraiser and cabinet maker, as did Joseph Topp, doubling in coal and flour. Thomas Notten took the prize for versatility, however. He was not only a grocer but also a draper, baker, glover, leather-breeches maker and fellmonger (hide-salesman).

Many of these trades had apprentices in the village and these youngsters worked under stricter guidelines than any school of the time imposed. So in 1854 when James Gye was bound an apprentice to the firm of Samuel Draper to learn the trade of carpentry and wheel-wrighting the indenture stipulated that "the apprentice shall not waste the goods of his said masters nor lend them unlawfully to any; he shall not commit fornication or contract Matrimony; shall not haunt Taverns nor Playhouses nor absent himself from his said Master's service day or night." The master contracted to pay young Gye one shilling a week for the first year and to increase that by one shilling a week at the end of each subsequent year until at the age of 21 Gye would be receiving five shillings a week.

Walton's clothing and furniture shop was at the Parsonage Lane and High Street cross-roads (opposite the present post office) in 1901 and its sales catalogues show a competitive approach. "Strong, useful watches," were offered at two shillings and sixpence halfpenny. "Bed quilts very slightly soiled" were on sale at a shilling and three farthings each. Children's coats "worth eight shillings and 11 pence" were on sale for five shillings less. Men's laced boots were priced at four shillings and six pence.

Misleading information brought one young would-be entrepreneur from Reading, Berkshire, to Market Lavington in mid-century. This was James Neate, who had had a casual meeting with a railway engineer who had a map showing that the proposed extension of the western railway from London to Bristol would pass through the village, with the railway station to be sited in Church Street opposite St Mary's. Neate had raised the money to purchase a property in High Street by 1852 but before he discovered the true facts. Nevertheless he opened "The Brewery Tap," a small brewery in White Street which also supplied wine and spirits; and his good ale, in nine, 18 and 36 gallon casks, selling for sixpence a gallon at harvest time, was very popular. Customers were served through the window of "The Tap" and drank their beer on the pavement. Neate prospered but died in 1920 at the age of 91, after which, by wish of the family, the business was closed down and the brewery demolished.

This then was the strata - the "lord" (though no lord he) his relatives, the church hierarchy, the gentry outside the inner circle and the trades people and farmers, with the labourers in the background. It was not often that the strata shifted. There appears to have been only one well-publicised social earthquake and, in ways we can only guess, it marked the end of the old order as much as the coming financial crash and a clash of nations was to do.

AN INDICTMENT

The background to a confrontation in the Wiltshire press in late 1887 is unclear, but from thenceforth the unquestioned authority of the Pleydell Bouveries in the neighbourhood was lost. The assault on that authority was by Samuel Saunders (1815-1908), a member of an old west-country family.[63] By all accounts he was a true 19th century radical, being quite uncompromising and fearless in his confrontations with the establishment and its guardians. These attitudes he had inherited from his father, Amram, who, according to his daughter Anne Saunders had "large combativeness, but no destructiveness. The doings and sayings of the leading men in Parliament were thoroughly scanned and criticised by him during the whole course of his life. He was not of the opinion that politics - that is, the guidance of the nation - should be left to corrupt in the hands of bad men." Amram was the father and Samuel the eldest brother of a firebrand, William Saunders (1824-1895), journalist, newspaper publisher, at times M.P. for Hull and Walworth and member of the London County Council. William also visited the United States in 1877, and his book *Through The Light Continent* was praised by the Prime Minister, Gladstone, as the most

[63] The family owned a mill in what was then Market Lavington in the mid 18th century and kept it until Edward Pleydell Bouverie cleared a space in the neighbourhood in the 1860's and built his mansion. As Samuel Saunders' daughter Anne put it: In the wood above Russell Mill - in which we used to go nutting - the Rt. Hon. Edward Pleydell Bouverie, in 1866, cleared a space and built himself an elegant mansion. Thus established, it was of course his [Edward's] wish to have at his own command the immediately surrounding property and in 1868 Russell Mill was sold to him." Samuel was the fourth son of the miller Amram Saunders, who took charge of the village meeting in 1830 at the time of the agricultural riots. Samuel married three times. When his first wife died he was left with three daughters under three years of age. He was survived by his third wife who he had married at the age of 86. When he was 92 he was quoted as saying "I have never touched tobacco........ I have never made a bet or played a game for money...... I have never had a headache, very rarely any other ache...... slept soundly every night and never been in bed one whole day from necessity."

interesting book he had read on America. The emigrant brother, Alfred Saunders, became not only an M.P., but the writer of an early history of New Zealand. Samuel was a teetotaller for 58 years and a vegetarian for 40. There is a splendid photograph of him in his later years wearing a trilby hat and frock-coat, a white beard to his mid-chest, standing in the midst of his family and employees, at his jam-factory at Lavington Sands.

It was Samuel who called a public meeting in his Workmen's' Hall on 1 November 1887. Though the Workmen's Hall was Saunders' property he made it available to his political opponents (presumably at a price) and there were a number of lively and overflowing political meetings there in the last two decades of the century. Following the 1 November gathering a public letter was delivered by a local Liberal M.P., Handel Cossham, to the Prime Minister, Lord Salisbury, complaining in the bitterest terms about Edward Pleydell Bouverie.

Addressed "From the inhabitants of Market Lavington," and signed by Saunders, the chairman of the meeting, it is worth quoting in full:

"We desire to draw your attention to the distressful condition which a large number of persons are living in this parish. We believe that the distress and suffering of which we complain are caused by unjust action of those who are entrusted by the State with the management of land. This parish contains 3,657 acres of land which is of excellent quality and capable of supporting a dense population. Nearly the whole of the land is under the direct management of the Chief Steward, or "landlord," the Rt. Honourable E.P. Bouverie."

"The whole of the parish is under his influence and control as "lord of the manor". Instead of seeing that the whole of the parishioners are as far as possible provided for, the Chief Steward has let 2,228 acres of land to one farmer. To make room for him five larger farms were put together, thus displacing five farmers and at the same time the number of labourers employed on the land was greatly reduced. Some of these labourers have gone to America and there produce corn and cheese, which are sent to this country and sold in Wiltshire markets."

"The wages of labourers in the parish are only nine shillings per week. Carters and cowmen work long hours on week-days and Sundays for 11s. 6d. a week. These men have to labour for about two-thirds of the amount which it would cost to supply their families with food only in the workhouse. Under such circumstances men, women and children must be living in a state of semi-starvation."

"This condition of things is distinctly caused by the methods adopted by the chief steward of this parish. The land in this district is capable of maintaining a family in great comfort on every five or ten acres. Such is proven to be the case by the fact that a number of families are living on these quantities of land, although they are charged per acre four times the rent and taxes paid by the large farmer."

"The 2,228 acres occupied by one man are rated at £1,078 ten shillings, or 9 shillings and sixpence an acre. The 481 acres in small holdings are rated at £906 12 shillings, or 37 shillings and five pence per acre. As the rate is founded upon the rent it follows that small owners pay in rent and rates four times as much as the large farmer. If they had land at the same rent they would enjoy abundant prosperity instead of suffering from penury and excessive labour."

"While small occupiers have thus been oppressed, the large farmer has not prospered. Immediately after the last harvest the chief steward, on his own behalf, seized all the crops, stocks and implements for arrears of rent, and now carries on the farm after discharging ten labourers of the few employed; thus adding to the distress of the population."

"It appears that of the capital which the larger farmer brought into the concern all the money which he borrowed from his friends has been lost. Thus the farmer has lost his time and capital, the labourers have worked and starved, while the Chief Steward has looked on and profited."

"It would be difficult to find a more sober, industrious and law-abiding population than that of Market Lavington. The chief desire of the people is to exercise their industry and enjoy the results thereof. This is denied them."

"From the steady habits and industrious character of the people, they add to the population at a rate considerably greater than they are removing by the calls of nature. No arrangements are made by the Chief Steward to meet this natural increase of population, although it would be easy to provide land for least 300 more families. The total population, instead of increasing, has diminished, and people are compelled to seek work elsewhere. These are great hardships, for in no part of the world is the soil or climate better adapted to the support of human life than in Wiltshire."

"The Chief Steward seems to do all in his power to drive away the people. Policemen, who are not paid but are controlled by him, are employed to prevent children from playing in the Market Place. They are instructed to seize and summon men who gather nuts or blackberries in the woods formerly open to the public. Spaces previous used as playgrounds have been enclosed. Fox cubs are imported and turned out in the woods adjoining land occupied by small farmers."

"These efforts to make a waste and a wilderness are carried out in the centre of the county which might produce sufficient food to feed a million persons besides its own population and in which there might be created a trade demand which would bring prosperity to manufacturers, merchants, and shopkeepers. The administration of the land must always be a chief concern of the Government, and no one can have

Maypole dancing in the Park, now the site of Lavington School.
The maypole was mounted on a cart and Mr Arthur Potter is holding the horse.
Among the dancers are members of the Oram, Potter, Baker, Maynard and Cooper families.

Mrs May Elisha introducing some of her pupils to her domestic animals.
A photograph (taken during the Second World War) which was featured in *Farmers Weekly*.

Market Lavington Prize Silver Band in 1911, outside what was then the Vicarage in the High Street. The bandmaster was Mr John H. Merritt.

The Market Lavington section of the National Reserve, in 1915.

control of the land except in accordance with the regulations of the Government."

"From the unjust sufferings of the people in this and adjoining parishes it is clear that either the principles or the methods of land administration are unwise and unjust. We therefore appeal to you, as the head of the Government, to take such measures or to propose such legislation as may be calculated to lessen and remove the evils of which we complain."

"Signed on behalf of the inhabitants of Market Lavington in public meeting assembled. 1 November 1887."

The first impression this overwrought and repetitive diatribe gives is that those who penned it did so out of desperation, but while this may be true of some of those present there was nothing uncalculating about Samuel Saunders. He was as shrewd and as highly combative as his father Amram had been, so there must also have been some personal enmity between himself and the "Chief Steward" which coloured his actions. But that said, he could scarcely speak for his fellow villagers without their consent and most of these were tenants, with very limited tenant rights, of the very man they were accusing of dictatorial and shady practices and of failure as a landlord and as a human being. They knew him to be fully capable of a hard response, but clearly as members of a community they felt, or had been persuaded to feel, that they had very little to lose.

This, of course, raises the question of what actually sparked the appeal to the Prime Minister. Some clues can be found in a confrontation nearly a month earlier during a Radical Party meeting at the Workmen's Hall between William Saunders and Edward Pleydell Bouverie's eldest son Walter. The Radical candidate, J.W. Phillips (who failed in his bid to oust the Liberals from their seat in West Wiltshire in the upcoming election) came in for some trenchant heckling when he attempted to discuss rural distress in Ireland. There were calls to "do something about England not Ireland: we are being put down ten times worse than the Irish."

Interrupting, Walter Pleydell Bouverie, a Liberal in the conservative mould like his father, asked how landowners were supposed to keep land in cultivation and raise agricultural wages.

William Saunders then asked: "Will you give your tenants the same protection as Irish tenants enjoy? There is no part of the civilised world where landowners can get labour as cheaply as Wiltshire. It is a disgrace to think that men earn nine or ten shillings a week."

Bouverie: "I would gladly pay 15 or 16 shillings a week if I could afford to."

Saunders: "If a working man could get land at the same price as farmers there would be no poverty."

Bouverie: "I would be happy to let to labourers land on the downs at five shillings an acre, but even at that price the land wouldn't pay."

Saunders: "The offer of five shillings an acre would do if let in perpetuity and the labourer be allowed to build a cottage on it."

Bouverie: "If a tenant farmer wanted valley land he'd have to pay £3 or £4 an acre. Ask any workman present whether he would care to go up to the down with a spade and dig up the flints." (Cries of "No, no.")

Walter Pleydell Bouverie held his own in this exchange with a much more experienced politician and the Saunders brothers must have been furious that by asking "questions" and by provoking argument he had effectively hijacked the meeting.

We don't know whether their fury contributed to their drafting of the letter to Salisbury, but we do know that when its contents was circulated it was Edward Pleydell Bouverie's turn to be furious and he called a large and well-publicised public meeting in the village within the week. Ostensibly Pleydell Bouverie was speaking in support of the Liberal M.P. William Long and he left his attack on Saunders until the last. In his wide-ranging if verbose speech beforehand Pleydell Bouverie named some of those figures in English history who he most admired: Oliver Cromwell,[64] William III, and William Pitt. He offered a succinct summary of his views when he said "The employment of the labouring classes entirely depends on the capital of those who have saved the means to employ them," whether the savings be by "themselves or by previous generations."

Then he turned on William Saunders. Pleydell Bouverie did not refer to him by name but only to his career as the owner of a news bureau, the Central News Agency:[65] "There is a person who lives in this neighbourhood who I see has been talking very much at meetings of what are called 'the unemployed' in London. I don't know why he has taken the chair at meetings of the unemployed, for he appears to be very busily employed himself (laughter). I fancy from what I have been told that he is connected with a thing called the Central News Agency which was shown up three or four years ago for being employed concocting false telegrams for the excitement of people. We know that he is employed in writing letters to the newspapers, very foolish ones, I venture to think (laughter). And

---

[64] Pleydell Bouverie said Cromwell was "One of the greatest men this country has ever seen."

[65] Pleydell Bouverie made ownership of this bureau sound a little shady. In fact it was a pioneer in its field - the first news distributing agency in the world and only a man of William Saunders' imagination could have made it so successful. In 1872 he persuaded the Dean of St Paul's to permit him to install a special telegraphic link in St Paul's Cathedral gallery on the occasion of the thanksgiving service for the recovery of the then Prince of Wales.

WILTSHIRE

Close to Lavington Station (G.W.R.) from whence London is reached in 1 hour 50 minutes.
Four miles from Devizes.

The

Lavington Manor Estate

An exceptionally attractive Residential and Agricultural Property of the highest
order, with its Valuable Manorial Rights, extending to about

2,500 Acres.

LAVINGTON MANOR HOUSE

is one of the ideal Country Seats of England, recently erected, with every
modern convenience.   Electric Light.   Perfect Water Supply and Sanitation.

Beautifully Timbered Park of about 175 *Acres*

13 Valuable Farms,

Comprising: West Park, Manor Farm, Little Cheverell, Littleton House, Hurst,
Greenlands, Cheverell Mill, Rooktree, Lime Kiln Farm, Knapp House, and others,

**EXCELLENT HOMESTEADS in first-rate repair; numerous ACCOMMODATION
HOLDINGS; 100 PRIVATE RESIDENCES and COTTAGES AND GARDENS,**

Comprising practically the entire Villages of

LITTLETON PANELL, LITTLE CHEVERELL & MARKET LAVINGTON.

Also Valuable Manorial Rights, Vicontiel, Quit and other Rent Charges.   Rent Roll produced

£4,125 per annum.

Messrs. FRANKLIN and JONES,

Will offer the above for sale by Public Auction on

THURSDAY & FRIDAY, JULY 23 & 24, 1914,

At the TOWN HALL, DEVIZES,

Commencing at ONE o'clock precisely each day.

Particulars with Conditions of Sale may be obtained from :—

THE LAND AGENT:	THE SOLICITORS:
W. ALEXANDER WILSON, Esq.,	Messrs. HOUSEMAN and CO.,
ESTATE OFFICE,	PARLIAMENT CHAMBERS,
LITTLETON PANELL,	GREAT SMITH STREET,
NEAR DEVIZES.	WESTMINSTER, LONDON, S.W.

THE AUCTIONEERS:

Messrs. FRANKLIN and JONES, F.S.I.,

ESTATE OFFICES : { FREWIN COURT, OXFORD ; and
{ CARLTON HOUSE, 11D, REGENT STREET, LONDON, S.W.

Page from Messrs. Franklin & Jones' sale catalogue for the Lavington Manor Estate, July 1914.

also I am told (for I have never read them) that he pens a great many paragraphs in newspapers which have only one conspicuous element in them, their complete absence of truth. How this man can be one of the unemployed I do not quite see. But still he takes the chair of a meeting of ragamuffins and roughs and not the honest unemployed working men and propounds to them as far as I can judge from newspapers, what his remedies are for the state of things in this country, where there is a deal of misery and suffering at all times, but still more just now when trade is very bad and agriculture is not profitable (hear, hear)."

"He tells them, as far as I can read in the newspapers: 'Oh I can double your wages. You shall pay no rates and taxes and half your rent and then you will be prosperous.' I wish I knew the secret (laughter), I should like to be one of the unemployed myself on those terms. I should like to pay no rates and taxes and half the rent paid and then I should take off my cap to the chairman of the unemployed meeting (laughter)."

"I do not know whether any of you have been to the theatre in London and seen an eminent comedian, a Mr Toole. It was a burlesque at one of the theatres. Mr Toole was Wat Tyler and he enumerated to his audience - I do not mean the people in the galleries and boxes, but to the mob who were on the stage - what he would do for them; how happy he would make them all, how they should pay no rates, no taxes, half their rents paid and so forth. This was the windup of his address to them *When Watt Tyler Is King*:

> "Paupers shall be fed on buttered crumpets
> And eat roast mutton to sounds of trumpets
> (roars of laughter)
> The poorest shall smoke Bengal Cheroots,
> And have another man to clean his boots.
> Someone asked: 'But what if the other man
> should make objection?'
> Well, then, upon reflection I see no other plan
> Than that I shall hang that other man."

Bouverie then continued: "I might suggest another couplet,"

> "Each lad shall have a lass both fair and stout
> Also a park in which to walk about.
> (laughter and prolonged cheering)."

Pleydell Bouverie was, of course, patronising his audience in the village, but he might have tempered his attempts at wit if he had a preview of the reply from his target, William Saunders, which the *Wiltshire Times* published immediately following its report of Bouverie's speech.

Saunders' letter to the editor read: "Wiltshire labourers who work for nine shillings a week can have but little (cause for) amusement and it is not surprising that they vehemently encouraged the Rt. Honourable E.P. Bouverie when he gave them his recitation of Mr Toole."

"Mr Bouverie has acted a part which will probably give a new turn to an historical reference. Instead of teaching the rising generation that 'Nero fiddled while Rome was burning' we shall tell them that 'Bouverie buffooned before his ruined tenants and his starving labourers."

"Mr Bouverie knew that his audience could not do otherwise than applaud, and he thus diverted attention from issues which he is totally unable to meet. Mr Bouverie as chief landlord has totally depopulated the parish, reduced wages, crushed the farmers and paralysed shopkeepers. Does he meet those charges by quoting Mr Toole?"

"He does not answer my statements by libelling me. The Central News is well able to defend itself. I discontinued the management of the Central News long before the date which Mr Bouverie names....."

"Mr Bouverie professes his obvious inability to understand the proposals made for the relief of the poor in London. Many people ridicule what they are unable to understand. My proposals were that men with small incomes should be exempted from rates as they are from taxes and that over-rented householders should have judicial rents, as in Ireland. That the great landlord of the parish should express his desire to have himself the advantage of such proposals shows to what extent Mr Bouverie carries his buffoonery."

We know so little about the underlying causes of this landlord-tenant confrontation simply because there was no representative village body at which villagers could air grievances. The first meeting of a democratically-elected body, the Parish Council, was seven years in the future. The plain fact was that the Pleydell Bouveries at the manor were able to do very much what they liked on lands they owned and, according to the Saunders' they felt they could do what they liked in areas not strictly under their control - like the village Market Place. It was, after all, the 19th century, which was enlightened certainly in comparison with those that preceded it, but very much still an England dominated by class and privilege. It is an old, even trite, story for its time.[66]

That said, the letter from the Samuel Saunders-organised village meeting is far from trite (if somewhat

---

[66] Here is a description of the "Third Class passengers," implicitly, for some, the lowest level of society in England before the First World War: "Their place in British society was well understood and had a long history. They were of those who in their little spare time formed the crowded and dingy background at all ceremonial rejoicings, past and present, from Royal progresses to public hangings; but their lifelong occupation was to till the land and mine the coal, to toil in the factories and man the ships, without whose labour in fact there never could have been a First Class Britain, and who were, in short, both the base of Britain's greatness and society's bottom. As such, ideally they should not be seen and certainly never heard." (*The Ship That Stood Still*, Leslie Reade, 1993).

overstated). It earned headlines in several newspapers throughout the West Country and it must have hurt the self-styled lord of the manor, who probably was as humane a landlord as any other in Wiltshire and a lot more compassionate than some. The hurt shows in his meandering, ill-suited response to Samuel's brother and suggests that in his later years at least - he was 69 at the time - Edward was no longer the astute politico. On the other hand he knew he had the backing of the majority of the county's press, notably the *Devizes and Wiltshire Gazette,* which was unashamedly conservative and anti-Radical.[67] It reported on the Bouveries with respect bordering on reverence and on William Saunders as a dangerous nuisance - at least until the day after his death.

Precisely what the brothers Saunders were seeking is unclear. Certainly Samuel was a spokesman for the village and what he saw to be the village's needs, but in the letter which undoubtedly he composed he was given to excesses of language and a combativeness which more than matched his opponent's.

What William Saunders was seeking is clearer. While his elder brother may have been content with an arena of village or even county politics, William, like Edward Bouverie who was a parliamentarian, was seeking national attention for his views - and getting it.[68] Within a few days of his sharp reply to Pleydell Bouverie he featured in the national - and local press - for having been arrested in London, at a major demonstration in Trafalgar Square, demanding the release from gaol of the Irish M.P. for Kilmainham, William O'Brien.[69] Later in the week the Government abandoned prosecution of Saunders because clearly it was unhappy about the legality of its actions in barring him and other demonstrators from a public place. But Saunders was not to be bought off and before the end of November 1887 he was in the news again, this time for speaking at a large rally in Hyde Park in which he was quoted as saying that the Government's land policy was unjust and causing poverty, depression of trade and unemployment.

So what was William Saunders really concerned with - Ireland or agricultural abuses? Both, it seems,

and we must look back to Anne Saunders' reminiscences in *Russell Mill* to discover that the Saunders' of Market Lavington were indeed deeply involved with developments in Ireland. She says of the death of the Irish patriot and agitator, Daniel O'Connell, in 1847, that her father had lost "an old friend (perhaps an exaggeration as they probably never met) and she quotes one of O'Connell's "latest convictions" as being that "the physical misery and social evils of Ireland cannot be successfully encountered by political [her emphasis] remedies."

The link with events in Ireland may have had some emotional overtones connected with the Saunders' natural radicalism, but the Saunders' also felt drawn to Ireland because of Irishmen like William O'Brien's overt and revolutionary views on land reform. Like O'Brien they unequivocally backed the National Land League of Ireland which came into being in 1879. The League's object was to persuade tenant farmers to organise to bring about reduction in their rents, to protect farmers threatened with eviction and to obtain "such reform in the laws relating to the land as will enable every tenant to become the owner of his holding by paying a fair rent for a limited number of years." In effect this would take land ownership out of the hands of the traditional landowners and give it to the tenant farmers. Samuel Saunders believed that this manifesto should apply to his native Wiltshire at least and the Saunders brothers wholeheartedly backed the first president of the League, Charles Stewart Parnell, when he said that "a fair rent is a rent the tenant can reasonably afford to pay according to the times, but in bad times a tenant cannot be expected to pay as much as he did in good times."

AN END TO ARGUMENTS

No response to the open letter to Salisbury appears to have been published, but there must have been some short-term reaction from Westminster and both parties to the dispute would have learned of it. In the long term there certainly was a thorough airing of the agricultural problems in Market Lavington and in the Plain villages via a Royal Commission on Agriculture with special

---

[67] On 17 November 1887 the *Devizes Gazette* said in an editorial that "when Samuel Saunders and friends take it upon themselves to brand by name a landed proprietor simply because that landed proprietor chooses to farm his own land, and do the best he can with it (in his own judgement) for the benefit of those around him, they are guilty of interference as unwarranted as it is offensive, and an interference which all right-thinking persons will repudiate!"

[68] In 1887 he was an M.P. for a second time. The Liberals had forsaken him at the time of the 1885 dissolution over his refusal to support Gladstone's proposal to exclude Irish members from the House of Commons, so he stood as a Radical candidate for Walworth and won the seat a year later.

[69] The size of this demonstration may be gauged from the forces of law and order marshalled to prevent its entry into Trafalgar Square - 5,000 police, with the first brigade of Grenadier Guards and the first brigade of Life Guards waiting in the wings. Later in the day, at a major clash with demonstrators, the Foot Guards outside the National Gallery fixed their bayonets and two squadrons of Life Guards moved in from Whitehall.

The corner of the Market Place, circa 1915, now occupied by shops, flats and part of Rochelle Court.
On the left, adjoining the shop, is the 'court' building once used for collecting manorial dues.

A gathering for the 1911 Coronation celebrations, with members of the Boys Brigade standing at the rear.

The 4th Wilts Territorials, in Church Street, leaving for camp in one of Sayers' 'buses, during 1913.
Jack Welch is on the extreme right, next to Bill Drury.

Mr Tom Haines was the last town crier in Market Lavington. Here he is at the village crossroads, circa 1935.
He always dressed in a smock and a top hat, and wore his medals when performing.
Also in the picture, from the left, are: Messrs. Plank, Burt, Sloper, Love, Hobbs and Buckland.
The two boys are Ken Buckland and Bob Drury.

attention to the Salisbury Plain District set up by the Salisbury Government in 1895.

By that time those who so bitterly opposed each other were dead, except for Samuel Saunders. Edward Pleydell Bouverie died at his London home, 44 Wilton Crescent, in 1889, but his funeral was at Lavington Church and was well-attended. There were five coaches of business associates and a special train was laid on for those returning to London.[70] The *Wiltshire Times* was circumlocute, as ever, in catching the style of the man - his opinions were "neither sufficiently plastic nor sufficiently cut and dried for some of his political colleagues," it said. "Personally, he was a most unassuming and charming man, full of reminiscences of another day than ours. He always had the full courage of his opinions." Translated from the diplomatic journalese of the time, the paper saw him as backward-looking and given to rigidity and dogmatism - in short well equipped with those Victorian values which have haunted the minds of some British politicians a century later.

His eldest son Walter appears to have been a diluted version of his father. Nevertheless he carried on the old man's quarrel with the Saunders at every opportunity and with some spirit. In 1889 he and Samuel Saunders fought for a seat on the District Council and Walter won by a far narrower margin than he had expected - by 402 votes to 339. By then his interest lay not in politics but in the prevention of the dismemberment of his father's little empire in Market Lavington. He launched Bouverie's "Best British Butter" with an appalling jingle beginning:

"Bouverie's butter is the best;
It takes the cake by every test,
In quality, price and all the rest,
It can't be beat."

But neither the product nor the versifying were enough to maintain Lavington Manor. Walter died suddenly in 1893 on the ocean liner *Umbria*, aged 45, on a return journey from the U.S. Reportedly, his last words were to his valet who related how Walter knew himself doomed, but he had hoped to have lived for seven more years to get his family back into their home - the Victorian manor-house. Certainly he was very heavily in debt. Another last word, again from the *Wiltshire Times*, is surprisingly frank: "Underneath a hot-headed

and fiery temperament there was a generous and kindly disposition." His memorial and to that of his wife, Katherine, who also died aged 45, is in Little Cheverell Church; they having lived at Little Cheverell Farm for many years.

The last to die was William Saunders, who returned home from taking a cure at Nice in April 1895 and died two weeks later at Samuel's Market Lavington house.[71] At the time of his death he held the seat of Walworth in the Commons with a majority of 205. He was also an office-holder in the Land Restoration League, advocating, as always, a more just distribution of property. He is buried in the south-west corner of St Mary's churchyard, a few feet from the grave of his old opponent Edward Pleydell Bouverie. The remarkable aspect to William is that he launched himself so late on a career of confrontation. He was demonstrating on the streets of London in his 60's. Perhaps he needed the late-19th century example and political philosophies of the Irish and the Russian revolutionaries to fire him.

ROYAL COMMISSION

Inevitably one of the chief witnesses before the Royal Commissioner, Rew, in 1895, was Samuel Saunders. Rew's examination of the agricultural problems in the villages around the Plain appears to have been exhaustive and he believed in first-hand acquaintance of the local community. He began with the premise that "there can be no doubt at all, that tenant farmers have lost heavily during the past ten to 125 years in the Salisbury Plain district." He referred to evidence that one owner of an estate of 1,500 acres was willing to accept offers of £10 per acre, including buildings and cottages, but had received only one offer in two years of advertising. He attended a Market Lavington meeting at which a farm-labourer gave evidence that farmers did not employ enough labour (precisely the claim in the letter to Salisbury) and the Commissioner noted that mention had been made specifically of one large unnamed farmer in the neighbourhood who, according to witnesses, did not use enough men in the fields. The farmer was present and the minutes of the meeting said that he resented this accusation "with considerable warmth."

The Commissioner concluded that relations between farmers and labourers were not satisfactory but

---

[70] He left the bulk of his estate, £91,627, to his eldest son Walter. He left £5,000 each to Edward Oliver Pleydell Bouverie and to one daughter, Eglantine; £750 to an unmarried daughter, Anne; and £250 to a married daughter, Ruth, "trusting that she is otherwise sufficiently provided for." Anne also received his Great Western Railway and Folkestone Water Works stock and "enjoyment for her life of 'the old house' at Lavington. She moved into it that year.

[71] The *Devizes Gazette* which had so cuttingly derided William Saunders for years said he had been "a man of remarkable adventure and energy and, possessing great ability, he achieved success in business and then made a name in public life which will not soon be forgotten." The *Dictionary Of National Biography* says of him that he was "One of the first English champions of the theories of land nationalisation," but it does observe that "latterly his views took too pronouncedly a socialist complexion for his Party."

he said labourers had to realise that farmers were in real financial difficulties. He quoted one farmer who was obviously concerned about strikes, that "the men have their heads up and would stir if they saw the chance, but they cannot do much in these flat, hanging times."

Figures before the Commission showed that the Wiltshire General and Agricultural Workers' Union had 1,800 members in 1895, with subs of a penny and a halfpenny a week out of a standard weekly wage of ten shillings, which farmers claimed was 14 to 15 shillings when rent-free or low-rent houses plus gardens and free potatoes were taken into account.

This brought the Commission to an examination of the labourers' cottages which Rew reported were, in the majority, "fairly good." At a small meeting of Market Lavington farmworkers Rew was told that the average cottage had two bedrooms upstairs and two rooms (one of them very small) downstairs with an average rent of £3 15 shillings to £4 year. One worker said his greatest problem was that he had insufficient rooms for his large family. The Commission learned that all cottages in the village were let independently of the farms and many belonged to small owners. The exceptions were the tied cottages, rented free or for a nominal sum to farmworkers in consideration of wages.

The Commission noted that there were many small holdings at Market Lavington on the greensand and that the soil was easily worked and well suited to growing vegetables and fruit. Inevitably Commissioner Rew was asked to look at model holdings and just as inevitably one of the model holdings was that of Samuel Saunders, who had bought six acres of land 25 years previously, building himself a house and then commencing fruit growing. Rew noted that at the time of his inspection Saunders was gathering 40 tons of fruit an acre, which was made into jam, jelly, syrup and "temperance drinks," or was preserved on the premises. He sold the jam for 30 to 60 shillings a hundredweight and had 1,200 customers, including hotels and business houses. He employed six men on spade labour all the year round at ten to 15 shillings a week from 7 a.m. to 5 p.m. Women who picked the fruit earned one shilling and threepence to one shilling and sixpence a day.[72]

Rew also saw a three acre holding "on the top of the hill" which he did not otherwise identify, which was rented at £3 an acre, with the cottage rented separately at £4 annually. The holding grew vegetables, which the farmer's wife took once a week 12 miles by donkey and cart to a country town. She also produced honey, which she sold at eight pence a pound.

Another farmer interviewed owned 16 acres and rented another 20 at £3 an acre annually and he complained of the difficulty of getting acreage at a reasonable rent. He said it was virtually impossible to pay three pounds an acre and make a living.

On a more general note Saunders took the Commissioner and the hearings aback by suggesting that land in Wiltshire at least should be nationalised and the Commission was even more surprised when two others at the hearing said the same. Saunders returned to his earlier complaints to Edward Pleydell Bouverie, when he supplied the Commission with figures which showed that 60 small holdings in Market Lavington occupied 128 acres, which were let for two pounds ten shillings an acre, while four farms occupied 2,890 acres and were let at ten shillings and sixpence an acre.

The Commissioner's overall finding was that "with any further fall in prices or with a series of bad seasons I cannot see how it is possible for the greater part of the land in the Salisbury Plain district to be farmed even in the most economical fashion. There are thousands of acres which are just on the margin of cultivation and very slight further pressure would lead to their being turned...... into rough sheep runs of literally prairie value."

END OF AN ERA

By 1898 the Pleydell Bouverie estate at Market Lavington was heavily mortgaged to the Wilts and Dorset Banking Company, 925 acres of downland was sold to the War Department and there were further sales later. The remainder of the estate, with some notable exceptions, was bought in 1902, by Charles Awdrey (1847-1912), a barrister and High Sheriff of Wilts, who was also a partner in W.H. Smith, stationers. Awdry bought the estate for £79,500, with the manor house let to the Marquess de Lavallette.[73] She died at the house in 1907, aged 85, but Awdrey did not move in until 1909. He did not have long to enjoy it, though it was estimated that he spent an additional £100,000 on it before his death in 1914.

The Lavington manor and other properties were again up for sale and the date, on 23 and 24 July that year, was just one of the many preludes to the end of the old order in Europe - and, for that matter, in Market Lavington. On offer were 2,500 acres and what the sales catalogue described, with the lack of estate-agents' reticence we associate with a later day, as "one of the ideal country seats of England, recently erected, with every modern convenience, electric light, perfect water

---

[72] The Saunders jam-making has left a profitable legacy to Easterton parish in the present day jam-factory. After Saunders' death his business passed to Cedric Gauntlett, son of another teetotaller, William Gauntlett. Cedric taught the trade to Samuel Moore and he founded the business which still continues.

[73] Georgina Gabrielle de Flahault, was born an English subject. She was the younger sister of the 4th Marchioness of Lansdowne. In 1871 she married the Marquis de Lavalette, who was at one time French Minister of Foreign Affairs and Ambassador to London.

An 'Our Day' sale held in the Market Place, in 1915, to raise money for the Red Cross.

Another view of the 'Our Day' sale for the Red Cross, in the Market Place, 1915.

supply and sanitation, beautifully timbered park of about 175 acres and 13 valuable farms." These were listed, in part, as West Park, Manor Farm, Little Cheverell, Cheverell Mill, Littleton House, Knapp House, Hurst, Greenlands, Rooktree and Lime Kiln Farm. In addition there were 100 private residences and cottages and gardens and "practically the entire village of Littleton Pannell and Little Cheverell as well as Market Lavington itself. The rent from these riches produced £4,125 a year - say £150,000 in the later 20th century. Knapp House Farm, of 122 acres, which had been let to James Watts at £155 a year, was passed in at £2,700. Miss Bouverie purchased 11 acres of beech woods on which timber was reserved, for £100 and two acres of meadow adjoining the woods for £60. A pair of cottages with gardens in White Street with an annual rent of £11 ten shillings sold for £210.

During the First World War the War Department authorised the cutting down of most of the woods and plantations on the estate, with much of the timber going to France for trench-props. In 1928 the manor house was again up for sale but there was little interest. Dauntsey's School acquired it for just £4,800 - a little more than the estate had brought in annually 14 years before. The only other bidder was a junk merchant who had plans to demolish it and sell off what he could.

Exempt from the 1914 and 1928 sales was the Old House, which by that time was home for two unmarried children of Edward the M.P. They were Edward Oliver (1856-1938) and Anne (13 March 1843 -13 August 1940). They lie beside their parents Edward and Elizabeth Anne, and their niece, Janie (1867-1870), in Market Lavington churchyard under unostentatious gravestones. Janie, born at Coleshill and dying in London, was the daughter of Anne's closest sister, Eglantine, and her husband Sir Augustus Frederick Stephenson. "A very happy little girl," says her epitaph.

Edward Oliver was the youngest child of eight. In their younger years Edward and Anne lived before the Manor was built at Little Cheverell Rectory or in London. The national Census in 1851 suggests the Old House, Anne's future home, may have been empty. By 1881, however, the widow and family of the village vicar Thomas Pearson, originally of Sparshoot, Buckinghamshire, had moved there from 18 High Street and she and her family probably remained there until Anne began a half-century occupancy in 1889. She was aged 47. The 1891 Census notes her London birthplace and that she he is named head of house, single, and "living on own means." Staying with her at the time of the Census was seven-year-old Pleydell Keppell Stephenson, her nephew and the brother of the long-dead Janie. Her brother, Edward Oliver, was probably living there also but was absent for the census.

Anne is still remembered by one or two villagers as "Gentle Annie," their link with a long-faded but more elegant world, but she remains an elusive figure.

She is described as a small, very slim woman and a photograph of her taken in the garden of the Old House, soon after the turn of the century, shows a fine-boned, elderly lady, elegantly if inappropriately dressed for wheeling her garden barrow. About 1920 a young observer of her, who lives today as a somewhat older neighbour of the Old House, recalls seeing her looking over her garden wall, wearing a black bonnet, black silk dress and holding a black umbrella. Others in the village recall the times when she held open days for the walled garden which, in later years at least, must have become her world. She had some more or less regular contact with the villagers through the so-called "Laying-in Society" which loaned sheets and baby clothes for confinements and certain items of clothing were given to the parents of the newly-born child. She must have had considerable resources of character as for much of her life she lived alone in a large house with only servants for company. Not of the mainstream of Bouveries she seems to have chosen to keep her distance from them - and they from her. In a family history dated 7 March 1930, the words, written in a crabbed but legible hand by Anne's brother Edward, are an unconscious obituary on the presence of the Pleydell Bouveries in the Market Lavington area: "The house in which Miss Bouverie lives was part of the estate and is her property, which is the only portion of the old holding remaining in the hands of members of the family." Today the only overt reminder of the Bouveries at the Old House are the elegantly-entwined initials E.P.B. and the words "restored 1873" carved over the porch.

Anne lived until her 97th year, but she withdrew more and more from village affairs in later years and is said never to have recovered from the death in 1930 of her chosen heir, her beloved nephew. Her funeral on 15 March 1940 was private to the extent that press coverage of her death was withheld until after her interment. Her death provided the Army with an opportunity to quarter soldiers in the Old House and to make full use of the spacious barn adjoining it. More than 30 soldiers lived in and around the property throughout the war, and after it ended the Radnor estate sold it to a farmer, Henry Davis, who lived at Knapp Farm, Market Lavington. The barn became very dilapidated but was reconditioned and the thatch replaced by an asbestos roof in 1953.

MORE VILLAGE LIFE

Housing and development has preoccupied the village for at least a century and a half. In 1845 the parish was seriously embarrassed by the condition of the property owned or leased out by the Church. A vestry meeting presided over by Amram Saunders (who else?) resolved unanimously that all the houses belonging to the parish should be sold as soon as possible and by auction. At a later meeting Admiral Bouverie said that some of the houses were in a very bad state of repair and on these the rents were very irregularly paid. Examples were numerous: six houses for which the rent per house was two pence a week, and of another 15 the highest rent was a shilling. The parish learned subsequently that it had spent more than £77 over the previous four years for a rent return of about £32. Anticipating perhaps that it would be difficult to sell cottages which were literally falling down, the vestry passed a motion which said: "...... as the advanced state of society requires that the houses of the poor should be kept in better repair than formerly and the present state of many of the houses being such as to engender weakness and disease, they (the vestry) recommend that some of the houses be pulled down immediately and the land let for gardens, that others be pulled down on the death of the present occupiers, and that the remainder be put in proper repair." An attached survey of the properties revealed that some were "old and damp," one was "in ruins," two were "in good repair but had no privy," and others were "very damp and insecure." The parish decided that seven of the 15 should be retained by the parish and the rents of these should be raised from about £10 to more than £17. Charity, it seems, did not always begin at home - or in the Church precincts either.

Market Lavington's public life went on formal record in 1894 with the election of the first Parish Council. The Local Government Act of that year called for a council for all villages with a population of more than 300. The council replaced the parish vestry, which until then had levied a church rate and, from the 19th century, another rate for other social services. The vestry had also been responsible for the appointment of parish officers like churchwardens and sextons, and there was an obligation to serve as one of these - unless one paid to avoid the obligation.

The Market Lavington Parish Council has met several times annually since its inception and the clerk's notes have provided a good picture of a community concerned with parochial affairs but in contact with its larger counterparts at District and County level, living in a larger world of war and peace, mourning and celebration. The names of the first councillors - 11 elected from 24 nominees - were mostly from families known in the district for centuries - Selfe, Welch, Hitchcock, Canning, Lye, Oram, Gye and Grist, among others. Edward Oliver Pleydell Bouverie, Anne's brother, was the Council's first Chairman.

Samuel Saunders stood for election, but was defeated and the Council was soon to regret it when early in the new year, 1895, allotments were an issue. The Council took note that there were then 146 acres of them, plus 163 acres of small-holdings and 220 grown men in the parish who technically could qualify for an allotment each. The Council called on applicants for allotments to give their names to the Clerk of the Council, but it warned that the cost would be more than five pence for every 16.5 square feet and a quarter's rent would be payable in advance. Nobody applied and

Saunders wrote a letter to the Council saying that labourers refused to apply for the allotments on such terms. He said that the Council's offer was "more worthy as a manifesto from a syndicate of land-sharpers willing to...... exploit the labourers of the working classes to their own pecuniary advantage than of a Parish Council having at heart the welfare of the people." This amounted to a move for impeachment and the Council, well aware of Saunders standing in the community, reacted cautiously. It replied that it was not there to make a profit from anyone and its chief concern was to protect ratepayers from loss. The allotments issue went into limbo.

Soon after this the Council suggested to Saunders that he might like to hand over control of the Workmen's Hall in the High Street, which had been built by bequest of £1,000 from the late Edward Saunders as the Temperance Hall where villagers were encouraged to spend an improving evening at the cost of a penny, reading temperance publications in front of an open fire. Predictably, Saunders said that the Council, which was predominantly Conservative, could not be trusted to manage the Hall according to the conditions of the bequest.

An early issue which was to dog Council deliberations for many years was the condition of the natural spring rising in Broadwell. It was for many years the chief source of fresh water for the village - until, in fact, the installation of running water in 1937. So, when it became insanitary or "disgusting" as Councillors were wont to describe it, or when the Bouverie manor or Clyffe Hall increased their demand for water by the highhanded expedient of pumping themselves their full requirements, the village suffered. In the days when there was no Council to oppose them the owners of the two large houses had arranged a high-pressure supply by using water-rams which sucked available water down the stream. Occasionally the village Council had the temerity to protest this diversion of water - in 1921, for instance, the Council's clerk wrote to the manor estate asking that the rams be used only at night and later in the year the Council chairman said that so serious was the water shortage that he had taken it upon himself to stop the rams between 8 a.m. and 2 p.m daily. Further, and one suspects unnecessary, confrontation was avoided when it rained, but manoeuvring continued over the years and in 1934, when once again the water-supply to the village was failing, Lord Warrington of Clyffe Hall found it necessary to remind the Council that the use of the rams had been legalised in 1865. By that time, of course, the manor was gone, but demands by Dauntsey's School for water were as great or greater. A compromise agreed on the rams being stopped for three hours out of the 24.

The bizarre aspect of the "shortage," which has every sign of having been exaggerated by the Council, was that for several decades the District Council suggested that the village go over to an alternative - and more reliable - supply of water, but on each occasion the village Council rejected the idea on the grounds of cost. In 1935, after another stern reminder from Lord Warrington, the District Council once again proposed to a public meeting that it install a water scheme serving several villages and costing Market Lavington £5,732 or an annual charge of £521. The village Council would have none of it and a number of people, whose memories must have been exceedingly short, said that the village had never been without sufficient water and that in any case the village had an alternate supply in its 150 private wells. When there was the inevitable shortage of water a year or two later Dauntsey's School wrote a letter of sympathy, but the shortage did not stop 211 out of 259 households in the village voting against any District water supply scheme. The District Council responded with a public notice in the *Devizes Gazette* telling those who might be interested that Market Lavington didn't want outside water and the District Council took matters into its own hands by installing running water. The year was 1936.

The water shortages suggests that Lavington has had more than its share of droughts and water problems, but it has also had a fair share of violent climactic changes. On 2 September 1862 a storm cut a swathe a half-mile wide and two miles long through Easterton and the two Lavingtons which, in half an hour, filled the Broadwell area seven feet deep with hailstones, destroying gardens and crops. The village High Street was six feet under water for a few minutes and people smashed holes in walls to prevent flooding into their homes. The villagers collected eight cartloads of flints in White Street which had been swept down from the hill by the flood-waters, and 78 dead sparrows were found inside the church, which at that time was being re-roofed.

Wiltshire's great snowstorm in 1881 was long remembered as much for its snow as for the thaw which followed. The snow fell for 36 hours beginning on 18 January and among the 20 who died in north Wiltshire was a Market Lavington carter, named Farr, a very powerful and big man known as "the pride of the county," who, with another carter and a boy were caught with a team of horses in snowdrifts near East Kennett.

About a week later James Welch wrote to one of his daughters from his house in Market Lavington that "it is so very cold that I can scarcely hold my pen. It is getting dark, and I hear it has begun snowing again on the Plain - the skys and Barometer both foretell a heavy fall."

Years later, in 1976, Broadwell dried up in the famously dry summer, not because the ancient well had run dry but because the Water Board had sunk a borehole into Easterton Clay and was diverting water. Eventually, after protests, the Wessex Water Authority pumped about 40,000 gallons a day into the dry stream bed to keep the water flowing.

The role of the Parish Councillors was to concern themselves with village issues, but there was always the great events outside the parish. So in 1897, the Council decided to take up a collection to buy a recreation ground for the village in honour of Queen Victoria's diamond jubilee. There was not enough money for that, so the village settled for a dinner for the older folk and a tea for the younger. The dinner and tea on 21 June cost £51 and 500 adults attended the meal in Miss Bouverie's barn behind the Old House. They ate 700 pounds of hot roast beef, 50 pounds of cold boiled beef, veal and ham, five sacks of potatoes and 400 hot plum puddings. They also drank 500 pints of beer. Four hundred children went to the tea, held in Rackets Court, now Fives Court, opposite. Walter Bouverie and his sister Anne distributed medals, and Edward Oliver and Anne opened their grounds to the public. There was dancing in the barn and in the nearby field until 9 p.m., when many people climbed to the Plain to watch for bonfires and the weather was "splendid." Wadworth breweries supplied 54 gallons of beer, and 200 coloured lamps decorated some of the shops in the High Street. A few days later the aged and infirm of the parish had a hot dinner cooked at the Vicarage and served in their homes.

These festivities set a precedent - at least for another generation. Five years later, at the celebrations for the coronation of Edward VII, 500 villagers ate 500 pounds of meat and 240 pounds of cake.

THE LATER CHURCH

The 1862 alterations to St Mary's Church were quite extensive and were combined with the levelling and consecration of the additional burial ground, sold to the church by Edward Pleydell Bouverie. The fine old roof of massive oak had been obscured by a ceiling of lath and plaster and with the restoration the beams were revealed and left open. The whole refurbishment of the roof and part of the chancel, with provision for 80 further seats for the congregation, was completed within a year and the cost was £1,086. During the restoration, services were held in Miss Bouverie's barn, for long after called the Church Barn.

The additional seating brought the removal of the early pews, however. When the Bouveries first worshipped at St Mary's they had pews five feet high behind a screen in the chancel to help preserve their privacy and, presumably, their status. In 1890, let it be recorded, Edward Bouverie expressed his wish to sit in the nave of the church with the rest of the congregation, and the choir sat in the chancel. The Bouveries' chancel pews disappeared. Gone also were lesser pews which had been the subject of keen bidding in the past. There survives a copy of the sale by William Grant to Thomas Smith of a church pew in St Mary's in 1784 for the handsome sum of £10. It was "the first seat or pew on the left hand, upon entering into the said church by the

Troops marching from Lavington Station, up Lavington Hill, to Bulford, circa 1904.

Australian troops on parade in the Market Place, in 1916. The view looks north from the High Street.

**The bells of St Mary's Church were re-hung by Messrs. Taylor of Loughborough in a steel frame, in 1927.
Here we see one of the bells being lowered from the belfry. Joe Gye is on the left, next is Taylor's man, and then
the Rev. J.A. Sturton. The man on the far right is unidentified.**

great south door."

Re-cast bells were installed on 13 February 1877 with due ceremony. Cannon were fired and a group of clergy ascended the belfry steps to "inaugurate" the new peal. A lunch for 250 at the Green Dragon followed and the whole parish of about 900 had tea.[74]

In 1899 the organ was rebuilt and in 1910 it was moved from the east end of the south aisle, where it had been imperfectly heard in the chancel, to the south side of the chancel. While the workmen were re-siting the organ they unearthed the bones of a member of the Legge family. Charles Awdry, Lord Warrington and the Vicar paid for most of the 1910 work, and, at the same time, Miss Bouverie had the Hay memorial window re-sited.

The monuments in the church are notably of more recent date than the fabric, presumably because those dating from earlier times suffered the destructive zeal of the Reformation. One of the oldest monuments, on the north wall in a gilded oval tablet of wood, is to Thomas Tanner, clerk, who for 46 years was the resident minister of the parish, and died in 1718, aged 78. A more famous son, Thomas Tanner, the ecclesiastical historian and Bishop of St Asaph, erected the monument.

Market Lavington's oldest recorded inhabitant has a succinct memorial outside the church. It is in the wall on the south-east corner of the nave: "In memory of Betty Lambourn, who died June 16 1782, Aged 107 years."

The village's most prominent son, Thomas Sainsbury (1730-1795) has the most elaborate tablet - a female figure leaning on a shrouded urn supported by a pillar. Thomas was an Alderman of the London ward of Billingsgate in 1778 and became Lord Mayor of London in 1786. There are monuments, with appropriate heraldry, to John Sainsbury, died 1735, and another John, died 1736, commemorated with a black marble ledge stone at the altar. There is an earlier John Sainsbury, who died in 1704, named on a stone mural monument; and a Samuel Sainsbury, who died 1745, remembered on the north wall of the chancel.

The Legge family have 16 relatives named on three tablets and there are more family references cut into the church floor. The Bouveries, with their complex and colourful coats-of-arms, are resplendently recalled on a stone mural monument. The double eagle in black is the distinctive motif of the family and here it is quartered with the arms of Pleydell, with whom the Bouverie family became allied in the 18th century, and the arms of Balfour, who married into the Pleydell Bouveries in the 19th century. There is also a memorial to the Rt Honourable Edward Pleydell Bouverie and to his wife, Elizabeth Anne, both of whom died in 1889.

The most tragic is, however, one to John and Jane Axford of Eastcott and their four children, all of whom died in infancy and in the space of eight years - John, aged a year; Jane aged seven; Francis, aged four; and Anne, aged two. Their mother died three days after Anne but John lived on another 26 years.

Another infant mortality is remembered on the north corner of the vestry, with a slab to Emma, second daughter of Robert and Sarah Pile. She died, aged 21 months, and her memorial carries the sobering inscription: "The young may die shortly - but the aged cannot live long - Green Fruit may be pluckt off or shaken down - But the ripe will fall of itself."

One memorial mentions the death in 1927 of Mabel Kirke, wife of a long-time Consular official in China, who died at sea, and, as the tablet says, was buried at sea in latitude 9.23 north and longtitude 67.35 east - in virtually the middle of the Indian Ocean, doubtless on her way home or on her way back to China.

On a lighter note, beside the ever-ready bell pulls in the bell-tower is a proud reminder that on 15 February 1928 six bell-ringers from the village rang "A Peal of Grandsire Doubles..... 5,040 changes" in three hours and four minutes. There is an authority in the village who can explain the complexity of this achievement, which involved not only the six strong bell-pullers but the entire population of the village, aurally at least.[75]

THE CHURCHYARD

St Mary's churchyard is picturesque and it hides its secrets well. The oldest part has the best view - south towards the plain. Here are gravestones that have long since lost their inscriptions - some probably from the early 17th century, when, incidentally, burial was not cheap. Elizabeth Bower, who was buried in the cemetery, left detailed instructions in her will proved in 1618 which showed that the gravediggers were to receive 10 shillings, a large sum. She was, however, a woman of property.[76]

More recent stones, chiefly from the 19th

---

[74] The inscriptions on the bells before recasting in 1876 showed that the treble was cast in 1656, the second in 1611, the third in 1726, the fourth in 1680, the fifth in 1611, and the tenor in 1715.

[75] Apparently the Market Lavington achievement of 1928, pales before the 27 hours of continuous bell-ringing, encompassing 40,320 changes, in a Kent church in the 18th century, which must have provided a restless night for light sleepers.

[76] She left her god-daughter, Elizabeth Andrews, her furniture as well as £200 "resting in son-in-law Richard Halbrick's hands, and to the poor of Steeple Lavington 13 shillings and four pence."

century, are on the eastern and northern sides of the church, but all too soon there will be no room left, with or without a view, because, like the majority of British villages, Market Lavington has grown steadily but its cemetery has expanded only a little. That expansion came with the sale to the church of additional land in 1862. Selling were several of the more prosperous citizens - Edward Bouverie, Mrs Legge and Mrs Fowle and it cost the village £235 - a handsome figure. The church added another half acre in 1906 when it bought land for £75 from Anne Pleydell Bouverie.

The problem is an ancient one which earlier Lavingtonians solved by draconian means. Over the centuries soil was added on all sides of the church and this permitted interments above older ones. At some points - especially on the south side - there were several layers of burials and when, in living memory, one mausoleum was being renovated six intermingled skulls were unearthed. As late as 1902 a parish meeting proposed that "in future graves be dug to a depth sufficient to take more than one body," and this approach to overcrowding must have been taken, probably without discussion, much earlier.

There are less than 300 gravestones in St Mary's churchyard - only a very small proportion of the villagers who, over the past 600 years, have found a final resting place there. Parish records for the 215 years from 1622 to 1837 show that 5,366 people were buried in the churchyard and from 1818 to 1836 alone there were 496 burials. We are faced with more than 12,000 over more than 600 years, allowing for a lower population but a higher incidence of disease in earlier times. The 1852 Burial Acts gave local authorities new powers to administer cemeteries and to enlarge burial areas and to dispose of old graves if required, but one, of a decision of the Market Lavington Parish Council in 1906, was to give approximately those powers to the churchwardens. Automatic removal and relocation of old graves is not a policy, but one day there may be no other option if the pressure remains for village burials.

The most imposing mausoleum is on the eastern edge of the graveyard, near the Museum gate, and is to the Legge family, making their representation both inside and outside the church unrivalled. Near the Legge tomb is the mausoleum of Admiral Duncombe Pleydell Bouverie, who died in 1850. His other relatives

in the churchyard, Edward Pleydell Bouverie, M.P., his daughter, Anne, his son, Edward Oliver, and his grandniece Janie, are sited, side by side, far from their distinguished forebear and close to a walkway on the far west side of the churchyard.

A curious adjunct to the cemetery is the so-called Bier House, where until recent years coffins were laid preparatory to burial. Mrs Hay of Clyffe Hall donated a bier to the parish in 1881 and had the Bier House built for it. After the person's death and lying in at home the funeral personnel moved the coffin (on a trolley) to the Bier House where it remained until burial. It is only since about 1970 that coffins have been taken to a mortuary before burial.

THE FIRST WORLD WAR

Market Lavington heard no shots fired in anger through the First World War but newly recruited soldiers and professional army men from the village marched away and some did not come back. There are 18 names on the First World War memorial in the churchyard and 19 on the memorial within the church. The Second World War memorial has 10 names.

Two memorials in the church to men who died in the wars are not included, presumably because they were not born in the village.[77] There is, however, a separate memorial to a village man, Percival Lorenzo Oram, only son of William and Louisa Oram, who died on 31 July 1917, aged 20.[78]

The village fought its war in the fields around the village because, nationally, food production was of prime concern. The shortages were severe at times, particularly in the 1939-45 war blockade years, and these shortages continued into peacetime.

National fervour about the war came to Wiltshire and Market Lavington in January 1915 when the regrettably jingoistic editor of a county newspaper, the *Weekly Dispatch,* asked the Parish Council for the number of men from the parish who were in the armed forces. The editor said he intended to award a medallion to the village showing the highest percentage. There is no record of the Council having supplied this information. The Council could have boasted of the contribution to the war effort of the Hiscock family - with all five sons in the army, following a tradition which saw three Hiscocks in the

[77] 2nd Lieutenant Augustus Montague Sargent, 15th Battalion Sherwood Foresters, was the grandson of Robert Wadman, of Market Lavington. He died on 7 April 1918 from wounds received in Aveluy Wood. "His tired body was laid to rest in the military cemetery of Doullens, 28 April 1918, aged 34 years," says his memorial tablet on the north aisle. The memorial to Captain Claude Richard Kirke, Captain in the Rajputana Rifles, Indian Army, does not link him directly or indirectly with the village. The eldest son of a civil servant who lived and worked in China, where Richard was born in 1906, he was mentioned in dispatches while on service in the Western Desert and died of wounds in Libya on 6 December 1941. He is buried in the military cemetery at Halfaya Sollum, Egypt.

[78] Among the names recorded on the group memorial is that of Harold Frederick Giddings, Military Medal, born in Urchfont and enlisted in Market Lavington, a lance-corporal in the Wiltshire Regiment, who died in action in Flanders, France, six days before the Armistice, on 5 November 1918.

Crimea in 1854-1855, and two others in the Peninsula War under Wellington.

There is a photograph in Market Lavington Museum, taken on 24 November 1915, which captures some of the atmosphere in the village at this stage of the war. It commemorates "Our Day," which aimed to "help at the Front the wounded from Home and Overseas." The photograph, taken at the corner of what is now the pharmacy (Briants Tobacconist and Retailers then) and looking north into Market Place, shows a Red Cross nurse, wearing a long white skirt onto which a red cross has been sewn, standing with a baby and a pram. Boys and girls are grouped among rows of sacked produce - potatoes, cauliflowers and cabbages, presumably brought in as gifts from neighbouring gardens and allotments. On the east wall of the Market Place buildings, beside a draped Union Jack, a lamb carcass and six hares are hanging, and upon the iron railings along the north side of the square there are framed paintings, presumably also donated for sale. Outside Briants there is a billboard which says "A public auction sale will be held in the Parish Room, Wed. at 1 p.m: violin. bicycle. sew machine. pig. lamb. hay, straw, roots, wheelbarrow, rabbits, poultry, fruits and vegetables etc., etc., etc." [see page 99].

By late 1915 blackout regulations - the so-called Lighting Order - were in force and the village was a quieter place than it had been for centuries. The village constable was responsible for seeing that all windows were screened and in October that year he reported one resident for a particularly blatant display of front-room lighting - by kerosene lamp as there was no electricity in the village then - in the Market Place - for which offence she was fined five shillings.

The village peace was disturbed violently once that year, however, when it was bombarded, not by Britain's enemies across the Channel, but by the artillery practising on Salisbury Plain. Shells fell in and around the village. There was no mention of casualties, but the village Council was most upset and sent a letter of protest to the War Office. Curiously, the *Devizes Gazette* did not report on this misplaced targeting, though it had ample room for reports on less potentially lethal broadsides at Council meetings.

Throughout both wars Market Lavington was a staging post for thousands of servicemen on their way to the war zones. Canadians and Australians stationed on or near the Plain marched through the High Street, and some remembered the friendliness of the villagers and came back for short leaves. One Canadian who did was Sapper James Augustus Williams, of the 3rd Tunnelling Company of the Canadian Army, stationed in Wiltshire and later in France, who married a Market Lavington girl. When he learned she was expecting their first child late in February 1916 he overstayed his leave. The local constable called at their house in Church Street on 9 March - eight days after he was due to report for shipment overseas - and later that day he

did report for duty. There is no record of his fate.

English soldiers also formed new relationships in the village. One was Private James Brinden Bell who married a local girl, at St Mary's, in January 1916 and set up house with her in No.8 the Market Place, during his final leave. In his absence she found he had a wife waiting for him for the previous four years in the north of England. He returned home to a six month gaol sentence.

The war years brought inflation, with wages failing, as usual, to keep up with prices. Prices in 1917, for instance, were 90 per cent higher than in 1914, but wages in Wiltshire were only about 50 per cent higher. One positive result was the introduction of a national minimum wage of 25 shillings a week in 1917 and by 1920 this had risen to 42 shillings (by which time prices were three times higher than six years earlier). Male manual labour was at a premium of course, with literally millions under arms and the work load fell on women, boys and elderly men. A 1918 report, which appalled many, revealed that the school laws requiring attendance in Wiltshire and some other counties had been suspended for the duration of the war, thus permitting boys aged 11 who had achieved the fourth standard of primary school not to continue classes. Many local schools ended classes for the day at noon on occasion and the children often worked in the fields or on casual jobs in the village for a three-halfpence an hour.

The Armistice and also the celebrations which followed it are unrecorded in the Market Lavington Parish Records, but in 1919 the Council supported a proposal that a record should be kept of those who had fought in the war and this list should include the names of those Canadian soldiers who had stayed in the village. The following year Lord Justice Warrington, of Clyffe Hall, undertook to compile a list of the Canadian soldiers who had been stationed in Market Lavington and who had died on the western front.

There were long term irreversible results of the years of war, and not just in villages like Market Lavington, but nationally. The big estates, which were tottering just prior to the eve of war, continued to decline. The motor vehicle brought an end to jobs for grooms, coachmen and helpers, and great gardens lost their little armies of gardeners. On the land, farmers who had prospered briefly, found they could not make ends meet and one of their expenses, church tithes, came under scrutiny. Many refused to pay (saying they quite literally could not) and bitter were the comments and scenes as bailiffs seized moveable property. One quote from a west country farmer summed up the view of many: "It's 'dearly beloved brethren,' on Sunday and confiscation of corn stacks on Monday." Caught in the middle were the clergy, whose income had been guaranteed centuries before by church-state agreements. These agreements came to an end in 1936 with legislation which provided ultimately for the end of the obligatory tithe rent charge.

The war remained fresh in the memories of some. The Market Lavington veterans, mainly from the 4th Wiltshire Regiment, marched to the churchyard for the annual Remembrance Day ceremonies and laid their wreaths. The Women's Institutes, first formed in Britain in 1915, flourished and became centres for women to discuss common problems free of religious or political bias. Market Lavington's Women's Institute was a lively one.

THE SECOND WORLD WAR

The first Council-recorded mention of a new war came in 1939 when the District Council - not the Parish one - decided, as the world staggered towards a fire-storm of unprecedented proportions, to disband the Lavington and District Fire Brigade. There was a furore and letters were sent to the Home Secretary, and the local Air Raid Precautions Officer said it was absolutely ridiculous to think of scrapping the fire engine. The District Council backed off and by 1940 it was bending over backwards to provide the Lavington District Fire Brigade with uniforms, new equipment and even a touch of paint for the Engine House.

The Second World War found Market Lavington safely away from urban targets, but on many a night villagers heard raiders moving north-west on their way to Bristol, and when the raids were heavy they could see the northern sky tinged by the flames. Once more there were nightly blackouts - but this time the curtains over the Georgian windows shielded electric light. It had been installed in 1927 and it was probably a chink of electric light which brought the village its only air-raid of significance - on the night of 3 December 1940, a misty winter's evening. Villagers heard the droning of a single aircraft for some time before a stick of small bombs fell in a line running south of High Street and due west from the Fiddington end of the village. No buildings were hit and nobody was injured.

The village was, however, in the front line of food production and the strain was great on farms which were largely unmechanised. Villagers soon became accustomed to blackout curtains, dark streets and ration books, but the real change in their lives came with the influx of evacuees from cities targeted for air-raids.

The shock for some of the evacuees must have been much greater, as many houses in the village still depended on Broadwell or their own well water and there were still houses without electricity. Flush lavatories were few - the sewage mains were not connected until 1956 - and some of the outhouses were primitive and inaccessible, particularly in winter and at night.

The evacuees were often a burden for those families assigned them. One house-owner recalls being billeted with a young London boy plus an army Colonel and his wife, and having to cook for all of them. The Colonel and those officers who succeeded him were in charge of the Pioneer Troop of about 40 soldiers quartered on the Old House - then empty - in Parsonage Lane. At any one time there might be more than 60 evacuees - most of them children - and the Parish Hall doubled as a school for them. The older evacuees helped grow vegetables and a few felt they could manage tending hens and milking cows. Some returned to the cities, particularly London, saying they would sooner face the bombs.

Fuel was short and people made long trips only rarely. Push-bikes carried people as far as Devizes, but most of the folk from the cities depended on the village for their supplies and entertainment as villagers had for centuries. Men were away at war and the Land Army girls from all over England trained for a month in agricultural skills at Dauntsey's and were then put to work on the farms. A few of the Land Army girls, who were billeted with local families, stayed on after the war and some married local men.

There are few references to the rigours of the six years of the Second World War in the Council record. There is mention of the collection of scrap metal and to the shortage of coal supplies, but the real shortage must have been food. The Womens' Institute reported proudly in February 1944 that it had collected 215 pounds of nettles and other medicinal herbs - the largest amount of any Wiltshire village.

Long after victory, in 1947, the Council minutes refer to the distribution "as before" of "a second allocation of jam from the Colonies," and in 1948 the Council took note of three allocations of "foodstuffs from the Dominions," which were distributed "in the same way as before." Obviously these were shipments to a Britain which was still suffering from rationing and there was a direct reference to this rationing in April 1948 when, because of bread rationing, the Sainsbury's Bread Charity had a balance in hand of nearly £47.

There is one other chilling note in 1953, the year in which the Soviet Union made it clear it had the hydrogen bomb: the Council received from the District Council a circular asking for nominations for an Evacuation and Billeting Officer in case of war. For some reason this was passed onto the Womens' Institute for comment and a full three years later a volunteer came forward. The cold war also prompted another letter from the District Council in 1960, asking for volunteers for a Civil Defence Movement, but Market Lavington Council decided to ignore this request because, as one member pointed out, future warfare would not allow time to organise "emergency feeding."

The war and its aftermath receded and the next event of national importance to occupy the Council, though briefly, was the death of King George VI in 1952. A memorial fund and a whist drive yielded rather more than £3. The two Royal events of more recent times, Queen Elizabeth's Jubilee in 1977 and the wedding of the Prince of Wales in 1981, provoked

Army manoeuvres. Tanks at the foot of Lavington Hill, circa 1935.
The photograph was taken with a 'box' camera by Mrs Jordan from her bedroom window.

No.1 Section of No.2 Platoon Home Guard outside the Old House, November 1941.
From the left, back row: W.F.Perry Senr., H.Tippet, R.Francis, S.Reynolds, A.Burt.
Front row: J.Hoare, Cpl. W.Sainsbury, Lt. J.H.C.Horner, Sgt. J.F.Welch, W.Perry Jnr., and H.Edwards.

different reactions. The Jubilee was celebrated with a bonfire on Fiddington Hill, a fancy dress competition in the Market Place, distribution of Jubilee mugs to all children, a lunch at St Barnabas School for senior citizens, a sports-day, an open-air dance and peals of bells. For the Royal wedding the Council made a grant of £50 towards celebrations but councillors reported there was little or no enthusiasm for any observances. Three public meetings had been held at which the maximum attendance had been seven. The £50 was spent on a trophy to be competed for annually by Lavington Secondary School children.

PLAN OR NO PLAN

The village has suffered from depression and profited from booms, as part of a national trend. It has had too many houses and, more recently, not much or chaotic planning or none at all, which combined with ruthless development destroyed fine buildings which had survived for centuries.

As long ago as 1919 a parish meeting discussed "the housing of the working classes," in response to four questions put by the District Council. The village Council suggested that 13 houses might be condemned as below standard and said that there was no shortage of housing in the parish, as the 1911 Census had shown that there were less than four villagers per house. The Council did say there were available sites for building and later in the year it told the District Council that it should erect 12 houses on two sites, six on the north side of the Devizes road near Spin Hill Cottages and the other six near Spring Cottages. The District Council then suggested two possible house-sizes which might be suitable for the village - one with a living room, scullery and three bedrooms, and another with this accommodation plus a parlour. The rent for the larger house would be a shilling a week more. The first two houses were completed in 1925 and the village Council announced it needed 12 more, six of both types. All these were completed by 1932.

The Market Place was, in fact, a prime target of complaint for many decades and by all accounts it was sadly neglected. Rents were low - three well-built cottages with slate roofs in the Market Place produced an annual rental of only £11 a year in 1895 and this did not encourage renovation. One of the best proportioned buildings in the village, the maltster's house on the north side of the Market Place, was pulled down in the 1930's to permit a bus operator to extend the parking area for his buses. No objection to this vandalism has been recorded. Much of the problem appears to have been a lack of clear title as to who owned the Market square. The village Council attempted often to establish ownership with a view to repairs and there were discussions about condemned houses in the Market Place which had been occupied by squatters. By 1953 the Parish Council was, however, drawing the attention of the District Council to what it described as the dangerous state of Market Place houses and the following year the Parish Council "understood" that there were at least 50 condemned houses in the village and it decided to press for the building of as many Council houses as possible. In fact there were 21 condemned houses, of which 15 were empty. The District Council said it was surveying how many unfit houses there were in the area, but by 1959 the developers had moved in, new council houses had been finished, but the Market Place was, in the words of the Council records, "still a mess."

Interestingly Market Lavington's village Council was closed to the public for the first 79 years of its existence and very soon after it opened its doors it encountered criticism about its handling of the chief preoccupation of the village in later years - its expansion and the provision of public services to handle that expansion. The Grove Farm development took many years to resolve and it is worth pursuing this in detail as an illustration of the problems thrown up by local bureaucracy at all levels.

The proposals for development of the site as a community centre coincided with discussions with the District Council on long-term planning for the village. At the beginning of the 1970's the District Council suggested that the population of the village should be kept to a maximum of 4,000 over the next 25 years and that some form of light industry should be set up on the northern boundary. A village study was drawn up and in 1974 was approved, and this defined three areas for possible development. Area 1 was Grove Farm, area 2 was the valley stretching from Northbrook to Drove Lane behind the High Street, and area 3 was the land between White Street and South Cliffe Estate.

While the village Council was digesting this study and manoeuvring with the District Council, it went ahead, in 1975, with its own plan for a village playing field and, with commendable speed, purchased five acres of land at Drove Lane for £5,000. By 1976 the playing field, consisting of two soccer pitches, a cricket square and plans for a running track and the sports pavilion, was complete. It emerged later that the total cost was a little less than £19,000, of which the Parish paid nearly £13,000.

Meanwhile the County Council released its own plans for the Grove Farm development. In November it said that the Grove Farm estate was to be developed "immediately," at a rate of 40 houses a year for five years, but it made it clear that it would be ten years before money would be available for a clinic, an old people's home and a library. In 1980 the Grove Farm development layout was before the village Council and this consisted of 22 bungalows and 101 other houses. The developers were offering three quarters of an acre of the land for sale as a community centre and another acre for old peoples' homes but the offer was rejected.

In 1983 the County Council Planning Officer announced preparation of a Local Plan for the village and suggested that any village appraisal could wait until planning began. At the same time the District Council asked the village Council to what use it would put the community land at Grove Farm and it suggested that the village hall would not be adequate when the development went ahead. Perhaps, it suggested, the present site could be sold to cover part of the cost of a new one. Delay seemed to be in the air, people were becoming restive, and in 1984 a District Council officer met with the Council apparently in an attempt to explain the lack of progress. There were now two acres which could be made available in the north-east corner of the site for community development, he said, but the situation was "confused."

Another airing of the confusion came in 1985 without much result. In 1986 new developers took over the project and applied to build 38 homes but it emerged that the land around Grove Farmhouse was in the hands of others. The Council discussed purchasing it but someone pointed out that at one time it had been offered as a gift to the local Planning Authority for community facilities.

In 1987 the village took the initiative and sent the District Council a list of issues which it felt should be addressed, including, apart from resolution of the Grove Farm community area, those for more sheltered accommodation for rental by the elderly, adequate parking, tree planting wherever possible, landscaping of Broadwell and road improvements. The national building boom was well advanced and later in the year the village Council encountered a proposal to erect 46 flats, in a three-storey block, for sale to the elderly, on the high ground next to the church. It rejected the proposal outright, but much of the Council's time was being taken up with outline planning applications. In the midst of this, a District Council emissary informed the village Council that contrary to earlier indications, there was no master-plan for the village because the County Council had not set out "strategic aims" which would, in any case, have to be interpreted to suit the local situation. A draft plan could possibly be ready by 1988 and a strip behind the High Street on the north side of the village could be developed with, possibly, 150 houses. There and then this idea was rejected.

What did emerge in 1988 was discussion of a District Council "Structure Plan." The village Council decided to do a feasibility study to see what people thought they needed. A head-on collision between the village and the District Council came in mid-year when it emerged that plans were under way for a development north of the Market Place, at Northbrook, involving 46 homes and three shops, costing some £2,000,000. The village Council said the village had enough shops and it said a total redevelopment of the Market Place should be a condition for this development. The developers then offered an acre behind the High Street in return for support of their development proposals. The village Council said it would resist further development at Northbrook. By 1989, however, there were new developers on the site and a new offer - £30,000 to redevelop the Market Place. The village Council thought about it.

Meanwhile, amid a flurry of other applications, the Council turned its attention to Grove Farm once more and this time the emphasis was on possible sites for a new village hall or community centre. A village meeting found, to the embarrassment of some, that there was not much interest in a new hall, but fresh impetus came at a later meeting when it emerged that the Dalecare Centre had shown interest in buying the old one. In mid-1991 the Council learned that the Grove Farm developers were asking £150,000 for their site and Dalecare was offering £91,000 for the Village Hall site. The Council decided to go ahead with the acquisition of the Grove Farm site and dispose of the Village Hall. In 1992, 140 Parishioners attended the annual Parish meeting in April - a near-record and the village resolved that a new management committee would control the proposed new hall and, it was said, would seek grants and other support for construction.

BRICKS AND MORTAR

The ancient village of Market Lavington probably clustered around the first church to be built on the hillock, but by the 16th century the expansion was to the north, south and east. The backbone of the village is Church Street, leading into High Street, and at one time the small market place, now rebuilt, must have been approximately in the centre.

Market Lavington has fine structures spanning seven centuries. There are 20th century homes which are pleasing and well-built and which will be seen by future generations as examples of this century's architecture that are worth recording and preserving. Many of the red brick village houses which are predominant today are refrontings on older dwellings and there is evidence that several of the High Street homes built in the 16th and 17th centuries had jettied fronts.

The following information includes details taken from the Historic Monuments Commission's report on the buildings it lists in Market Lavington. Much of this report dates from 1972 and the Commission may have made amendments to its findings since then. In addition other qualified and informed people have examined village property and have provided some additional information. All structures mentioned are listed Grade II, with the exception of the Old House in Parsonage Lane, which is listed Grade I.

CHURCH STREET

The Vicarage. It has been the Vicarage since 1945. Circa 1710-1730. Flemish bond brickwork with raised stone quoins and dressings. Two storeys, cellars and attics, five bays. Central stair hall with flanking reception rooms and kitchen wing to right at rear. Central six-panelled door with segmental head and stone architrave. Flat stone canopy on brackets. 12-paned sash windows, also with stone architraves, segmental heads and keyblocks. Heads of ground floor windows raised to stone cornice. Boxed eaves. Roof hipped, with two hipped dormers. Interior has early 18th century dog leg stair. Bead moulded stone fireplace in left sitting room. Chamfered ceiling beam to right room, and a deep chamfered spine beam with bar stops to kitchen, probably re-used. Rear door is 18th century, panelled, now enclosed in 20th century domestic extensions.

No.12. Early 19th century. Rendered and whitewashed, tiled roof. Two storeys and cellar, three bays. Bays and floors defined by raised bands. Central half-glazed door with pent roof canopy. Four-paned sashes, those on ground floor replaced, within segmental headed openings. Gable stacks. Included primarily for group value.

Nos. 18-20. Two cottages in block. Mid-18th century. Greensand and rubble, faced with colourwashed brick on stone plinths. Tiled roof. Two storeys and cellar, five bays. No.18 on right has six-panelled door with 20th century gabled canopy and paned casement windows in segmental headed openings. No.20 has boarded door and similar windows. Roof half hipped left and stack. No.18 has a one bay rear wing with gable stack, rebuilt wider, and stack in re-entrant angle.

School. School-rooms built in 1846. English bond brick with stone dressings. Fishscale tiled roofs. 'T' plan with one classroom and service rooms in head of T, one double and one single class-room in stem. Main entrance, a four-centred stone arch with casement mouldings and label in cross wing. Second entrance in lean-to lobby on right side of stem. Two-light stone-mullioned windows. Capped gables. Octagonal chimneys and zinc galvanised roof vents. Timber screen internally dividing main classrooms.

Lying above the old school in Church Street is the **Museum,** which was the home of the school-master in the mid 19th century. Florence Shore, born in the house in 1908, was present at the opening of the Museum in September 1985. The Museum is, quite simply, a portrait of Market Lavington which no words can match.

No 33. House in row. Early mid-19th century. Brick with stone facade, slate roof. Two storeys and cellar, three bays. Lower half of front below guilloche plat band is line rusticated. End pilasters rising to eaves band and Ionic capitals. Central six-panelled door with doorcase of Ionic pilasters and flat canopy. Casement windows with sidelights; four-paned sashes over door

with palmette eaves brackets either side. Roof hipped.

HIGH STREET (NORTH SIDE)

No.1 (The Post Office). House at end of row, formerly a bakery. 17th and 18th century. Rendered, with tiled roof. Two storeys, three bays. 19th century shallow bay shopfront at centre with half glazed door all under corniced fascia. 16-paned sashes with segmental headed openings and stone sills. 18th century stack to right in rear pitch of roof and a rebuilt external stack to left gable. Slate lean-to across rear with flat roofed dormer. Interior has chamfered ceiling beam to left bay without chamfer stops.

No.9. House, now a bank with a flat over. 16th or 17th century. Timber framed with colourwashed brick ground floor, jettied and rendered to first floor, and roof tiled. Two storeys, two bays. Arcaded shop window with recessed door in left bay. Four-paned sashes and moulded timber cornice. Building recorded as having jetties on both sides, indicating it was once free-standing. Two storey extension to rear with various windows. Second pantiled roof to rear. The oven for the earlier bakery runs under the rear garden.

No.11. Early 19th century, probably containing earlier work. Flemish brickwork, rendered on ground floor, slate roof. Three storeys, two bays. Entrance off-centre, a five-panelled door with fanlights in deep reveals. Large 20th century bow window. 12-paned sashes to first floor with gauged brick lintels, and six-paned sashes to second floor. Parapet rebuilt. Stack on left in low pitched roof. Included primarily for group value.

No.13. 17th century, refaced early 19th century. Rendered, with slate roof. Two storeys and cellar, three bays. Central five-panelled door with overlight in pilastered and gabled surround. Eight-paned shop window to left with flaking pilasters and consoles. Tripartite window to right. Plat band. 12-paned sashes with concealed boxes to first floor. Gable stack to right. Interior has exposed timber framing and ceiling beams.

No.35 (Greystones House). House with office. Early 18th century. Rendered greensand, with tiled roof. Two storeys and cellar. Three bays. Central stair hall, flanking reception rooms and rear wing on left with dining room and kitchen. Central panelled door in round arched opening. 12-paned sashes, and Venetian windows to both floors in east gable end. Lean-to block at east end, now office, probably a survival of an independent 17th century house. Kitchen in rear extension has early 19th century Gothic ogee headed timber and leaded window. Interior: Timber-framed partitions to hall. Early 19th century dog leg stair with stick balusters and brackets to treads. Rear wing has angle fireplace, early 18th century cupboard with wavy splat vent over, and ogee stops to chamfered spine

The Young Farmers in the High Street, in 1941, with the school headmaster Mr Stowe.
The children include members of the Baker, Huxtable, Jenks, Wells, Francis,
Gingell, King, Sheppard, Perry and Ellis families.

1953 Coronation celebrations included a football match "Married versus Singles". The referee is Stan Cooper.
Back row, from the left: the Misses Baker, Razey, Gale, Oram, Potter, Taylor, Ellis, Gibbs, Preedy, Hobbs and
Ellis. Front row: Mesdames Ellis, Askey, Elisha, Gale, Cooper, Razey, Jones, Baker, unknown, and McKinnon.

beam. This is repeated in cellar under front room. Office has deep chamfered ceiling beam with bar and octagon stops, and similar cross beam to cellar.

No.73 (The Studio). Friends Meeting House, now studio. 1716 and later 18th century. Brick, English and garden wall bond with greensand gable to street, tiled roof. Symmetrical five bay elevation facing east. Two pairs of panelled doors with Bath stone surrounds and arris roll. 12-paned sashes with segmental heads, five-paned to upper level balcony. Large 30-paned sash windows to gables of body of meeting house with segmental arch and keystone. Roof hipped. Interior has panelled front to balcony supported on four columns set on long axis. Central column supports flat ceiling and roof. Opposite front, a long narrow graveyard with some remaining headstones.

No.79. Early/Mid-18th century. Stone, faced in brick, with tiled roof. Two storeys, attic and cellars, five bays. Through hall plan with service wing on right, the re-entrant angle infilled, 20th century. Six-panelled door, the upper panels glazed with shell hood reset in this position. 12-paned sashes, not quite symmetrical. Valence fascia board and two early 20th century gabled dormers. One flush dormer to rear and kitchen wing with two small gables. Interior has good 18th century stair with turned balusters. Chamfered ceiling beams, that to left sitting room deeply chamfered, and cross beam to kitchen with bar stops. 18th century cupboards either side of angled fireplace in kitchen. Roof of four bays, principal rafter and collar trusses with butt purlins and threaded diagonal ridge. Stone cellar under right bay leading to segmental vaulted wine vault to rear.

No.85 (Ivy Lodge). Late 1700s and 1832. Greensand rubble with brick side elevations, slate roof. Two storeys, reducing to single storey and basement on right. Three bays. Central stair hall plan with kitchen to right, parlour to left, and rear wing on left converted to drawing room and second entrance in early 19th century. Re-entrant angle infilled with dairy, now general purpose room. Central half-glazed door within wide arched porch. 20-paned sashes, the upper floor having brick patching from an earlier scheme of fenestration. Right front added early 19th century, windows, etc., said to come from Erlestoke Manor, re-erected here approximately half metre in front of original end. This has central door within metal lattice porch, and flanking large 12-paned sashes and arched brick lintels. Roof hipped. Interior remodelled 1832 (new dwelling extension referred to in deeds). Left room of earlier work has angle stack and binder with stop and scoop chamfer stops. Main chamber above has similar beam with double leaf shaped stops, bar and pellets. Stair split to upper and lower levels, with high early 19th century drawing room with cornice. Front has butt and threaded purlin roof.

HIGH STREET (SOUTH SIDE)

No.6 (The Red House). Farmhouse, now house in a row. 17th and mid-18th century. Flemish brick on stone sill, with flush stone quoins. Tiled roof. Two storeys, cellar and attics, four wide bays. Central boarded door within moulded quoined doorcase, and flat canopy on stone brackets. Plat band. Three-light stone framed and mullioned windows to front, but two-light stone window to left of door, and the ground floor windows of bays three and four blocked. Hipped dormers to the two central bays. To rear, a stone mullioned and transomed window. Rear wing on left, single storey and attic, has gable stack and lean-to beyond. Interior not seen, may be of interest.

No.8 (The King's Arms inn). 17th century or earlier, and early 19th century. Stone, rendered to ground floor, with jettied and banded tile hung timber-framed upper floor. Pantiled roof. Two storeys with cellar, three bays, fourth bay on left a separate structure. 20th century six-panelled door plus 20 and 16-paned sashes to ground floor, timber casement windows to first floor. Roof hipped to right. Rear wing on left. The left bay has a steeper pitched roof. Double range rear roofs. Interior not seen.

No.10 (Kytes Cottage). 17th century. Rough casting on timber framing on greensand lower walls. Pantiled roof. Single storey and attic, raised to two storeys. Two bays, with entrance to through passage, now removed and rooms each side, being main living room to left, and unheated bay to right. Central four-panelled door, and large paned shop window to ground floor, three-light casement windows to upper floor. Gable stack to left. Brick lean-to extension behind stack containing stairs. Interior: Chalkstone stack with timber beam with run-out chamfers. Spine beam to living room has elaborate chamfer stops, pyramid, bar and raised octagon. Simpler chamfer stops to inner room.

Nos.14, 16, & 18. Block of three shops. 16th/17th century, refaced early 19th century. Timber framed, refaced in brick and partly colourwashed. Pantiled roof. two storeys, 2:2:1 bays stepped up hill. Various 19th century shop windows and doors, including square bay window to left half of No.16, and recessed corner entrance to No.14. This returns by two bays to rear, continued by a long range of attached buildings, not of special interest. Rear wing across Nos.14 and 16. Interior of left bay (No.16) has bar stopped chamfered spine beam, with cross beam in second bay with shaped scoop stops. No.14 is of separate build, probably a 17th century addition. Ogee stops to spine beam and inner wall of square bracing and wavy corner braces. Roof of eastern bay has straight windbraces to intermediate truss. Central bay originally single storey and attic has surviving truss at lower level with wattle and daub infill.

Nos.22-26. House and a shop. Early 19th century. Flemish brickwork with slate roof. Two storeys, three bays, double range, with central entrance and butcher's shop on right, long rear wing on left. Original six-panelled door over three steps, with fanlights set in painted reveals. Flat canopy on cast iron brackets. Shop window has recessed door on right, side panelled pilasters, and similar flat canopy on four cast iron brackets. Plat band. 16-paned sashes but 12-paned over door. Elevation and roof cranked to follow line of road. Roof hipped on return to rear wing.

Nos.26 & 28 (Green Dragon public house). Late 19th century front probably encasing 17th century structure. Flemish brickwork with fishscale tiled roof. Two storeys and attic, six bays, comprising entrance in fifth bay, a four-panelled door with Tuscan stone portico surmounted by a painted dragon. Late 19th century two and three-light windows to ground floor with stone mullions and paned upper sashes. Stone lintels and sills. Similar windows to first floor. Blocked arched window over portico. Secondary entrance, a half glazed door in bay two. One gabled dormer. Gable stacks and single flue stack to third bay. Rear wing partly tile hung. Left bay rendered and colourwashed. Interior: Altered. Main bar in second bay has ceiling spine beam and deeply chamfered ceiling beam to bar extensions in rear wing. Upper floors not seen.

No.30. House in row. 17th century. Timber framed with pantiled roof. Two storeys, the western bay of larger house now represented by Nos.30. & 32. Front rendered with brick bay with tiled roof extending over 20th century door on left. Upper floor has a six-light canted oriole window of 17th century with double billet moulded cornice and two long carved supporting brackets.

Nos.30-32 (Old Bell House). House in row, once an inn. 17th/18th century, front rebuilt after fire early 20th century. Three bays, with central door under pent tiled roof. Three-light timber windows with overlights and timber lintel shaped on lower arris. Similar windows on upper floor but without overlights. 18th century brickwork at rear, probably rearward extensions of original 17th century structure of which No.30 is the western bay (q.v.). Included primarily for group value.

No.34 (White Knights). An early 19th century house. Colourwashed brick with slate roof. Two storeys and cellar, three bays. Entrance off centre, a six-panelled door with fanlight, inset. 19th/20th century open pediment on curved iron brackets. Plate glass sashes to ground floor, that to left tripartite, with rendered lintels. Plat band. 12-paned sashes to upper floor with rendered outstepping voussoir lintels. Gable stacks. One bay rear on right, the lower section built in greensand, and two-storey wing on left. Like Nos.30-32, included primarily

for group value.

No.38. Mid-18th century. Malmstone, line rendered to front, with slate roof. Single storey and attic, raised to two storeys. Three bays, with added 19th century bay on left. Entrance offset, a six-panelled and fielded door with moulded architrave and flat canopy on cut brackets. 12-paned sashes with boxes set well forward. Stack to left gable before extensions. Extensions similar but lower pitched roof and sashes set in rebates. Three bay 19th century two storey brick wing added to rear.

No.42 (former Workmen's Hall). Now library with meeting hall over. Built 1865-1866 for Edward Saunders' Temperance Fund. Flemish brickwork with slate roof. Tall two-storey facade of four bays, with carriage entry in fourth bay. Entrance central to the three bays, with flush stone portico on four pilasters and attic bearing inscription and date. Bays defined by giant brick pilasters with stone caps, eaves and sill bands. 16-paned sashes with eared moulded stone architraves and cornices. Carriageway arch is of gauged brick with stone keyblock, and clock over with stone surround and dripmould. Gable stacks. Late 19th century two-bay wing on left. Rear elevation altered. Loading door over carriage arch and simpler 16-pane sashes. Dentilled eaves. Interior has the large meeting hall on first floor. Window shutters in reveals. The building was erected by the Temperance Society and provided dole of soup and bread pudding when needed. Included for group value, and as an interesting example of the confidence of the social provisions for the needy in the mid-19th century.

Nos.48-50 (Palm House). Late 17th/Early 18th century. Roughcast on stonework, with tiled roof and slated eaves courses. Two storeys, attics and cellars, two bays, originally forming the hall and inner room of house incorporating No.50 (q.v.). Rear wing, original kitchen, now sitting room, with present kitchen in lean-to extension of early 20th century on side. Central entrance, a six-fielded and panelled door in arris beaded frame. Flat canopy on shaped brackets. 16-pane sashes with flush boxes to both floors and two hipped dormers. Roof half hipped to left. Left bay contains entrance of No.50. At rear partly projecting stair gabled above eaves. Interior: Original hall with cross beams with check and hollow chamfer stops, now subdivided on cross-beam. Newel stair lateral to hall, with splat balusters at attic level. Similar ceiling beams at first floor level, with flying freehold over No.50. Attic also interlocking, with single butt purlin roof. Rear wing has large open lateral fireplace, largely rebuilt.

No.50. Late 17th, early 18th century, refaced 19th century. Pebbledashed stone and brick, with tiled roof. Two storeys and attic. Entrance in end bay of No.48, Palm House, to hall with drawing room to left and cross

Mr Max Greenwood (Headmaster) and Mr Brian Rees (Deputy Head), outside the old School, with pupils leaving for the new Primary School in Drove Lane. The old School closed in 1971.

stair hall before dining room and kitchen in rear wing. Six-panelled door and flat canopy on shaped brackets. 19th century 12-paned sashes to both floors, and hipped dormer. Roof rises to above No.48. and is half hipped to left. Interior: building probably represents parlour end of 17th century house. Hall with early 18th century pine panelling and fine round-headed 18th century display cabinet in internal wall to drawing room. This has panelling and shutters, and 18th century fireplace with Carrara slips. Stair has two turned balusters per tread, handrail and newel replaced by one from Spye Park, but original early 18th century handrail on upper flights. Stone fireplace to first floor, also 18th century panelling and shutters. Palm House, was used for a time in the 19th century by Dr Willett for his private lunatic asylum. This was moved later to Fiddington House because the central village site was both too small and the inmates were "too noisy" for the villagers, not, as one might have thought, the other way round.

No.52. 17th or 18th century, gable end to street. Painted pebbledash with pantiled roof. Two storeys and attic. 20th century panelled door to left and flat canopy with cut brackets. 16-paned sashes to ground floor, three-light casements to first floor and replaced two-light window in gable, which is half hipped. Interior has small front room, probably originally a shop, and large living room to rear with lateral stack, and narrower kitchen extension. Spine beam to living room has check and scooped chamfer stops. Timber lintel to fireplace.

No.70 & No.72 (Clay's Hill Cottage). Two cottages probably 17th century, enlarged early 19th century. Colourwashed greensand with upper floor in brick. Pantiled roof. Single storey and attic, raised to two storeys, three bays. Late 20th century doors. Three-light windows to ground floor in segmental headed openings, the left bay having window with timber lintel. Three light casement windows to upper floor. Stacks to bays one and three. Lean-to across right gable.

No.74. Late 18th or early 19th century. Colourwashed brick with pantiled roof. Two storeys, three bays. Central half-glazed door with flat canopy on brackets. 15-paned hung sashes in segmental arched openings. Gable stacks.

No.76 (Starlings). Early 19th century. Flemish brickwork with slate roof. Two storeys, three bays. Central stair hall. Four-panelled door in lined reveals and flat canopy on consoles. Large tripartite 12-pane sashes and simple 12-pane sashes to first floor, all with gauged brick lintels with slightly cambered soffits. Gable stacks.

MARKET PLACE

Tragically the setting of the ancient Market Place is lost to development, but by all accounts most of the houses flanking it had fallen into decay before the Second World War. Photographs from the early 20th century show imposing buildings on the east and north sides, particularly a fine malthouse on the north. A house on the east of the square, in which the manor courts were held for centuries and the market tolls paid, was demolished in 1961. Its replacement, modern housing known as Rochelle Court, is a reminder of the ancient usage.

No.4. The sole remaining early structure in the central market place of the town. 16th or early 17th century. Roughcast with pantiled roof. Two storeys, two bays. Mid-20th century door with slate canopy. Timber casement windows to ground floor, four-light painted stone-mullioned windows to first floor and similar timber window to rear. Large axially set stack to left gable with two diagonally set brick flues. 20th century lean-to at rear. Interior has major fireplace blocked, and two deeply chamfered beams.

NORTHBROOK

The Rest. Cottage at end of the street. Late 17th/early 18th century. Colourwashed greensand rubble lined with chalkstone, thatched roof. Single storey and attic, originally a single heated bay with gable stack, a second bay, now kitchen, added behind stack in similar construction. Boarded door with shaped head under thatched canopy. Small paned and timber casement windows. Bathroom extensions added 20th century to right gable. Internally, living room has unshaped spine beam resting on chalkstone open fireplace with replaced timber lintel. Probably oven removed when door broken through and second bay added. Roof of round pole timber and elementary pole collars. An interesting example of a surviving humble dwelling.

PARSONAGE LANE

The lane's close associations with the one-time Bouverie property, the Old House, brought changes in the 1860's. Opposite the still-standing barn (in the grounds of No.14. Parsonage Lane) the Bouveries built a rackets court and this was converted after the Second World War to a private home, now called "The Fives Court." In 1862 the Bouverie family also demolished the former Parsonage House which the family owned. It had served not only as a parsonage, but as an estate house and was the school conducted by the Saunders sisters (see chapter on Education, page 75). There is a sketch which shows it to have been a building of some distinction but after its demolition Edward Bouverie removed an elegant shell porch and a semi-circular stone door-step from it and built the shell porch into the wall surrounding the kitchen garden of the Manor House. Standing in place of the Parsonage are two fine semi-detached estate cottages.

No.5. Possibly 16th and early 18th century. Greensand,

with diaper brick facade with flush stone quoins on a greensand sill. Tiled roof. Two storeys and cellar. Three bays. Central stair hall plan. Elevation symmetrical. Central boarded door with ashlar doorcase bearing ogee moulding. Small brick arch and keystone over. Two-light flush stone framed windows with similar mouldings and timber paned glazing. Flat brick arch with keystone over each. Mid wall moulded stone string. Roof hipped. Rear wall has one three-light hollow moulded stone window with label over, seemingly in original position. Interior has 18th century stair with turned balusters and chamfered spine beams to flanking rooms.

No.7. Early 19th century, possibly including earlier work. Colourwashed brick with thatched roof. Two storeys, two bays. 20th century door on left and paned timber windows, all ground floor openings have segmental brick arches. Late 20th century half-bay extension at right end. Included primarily for group value.

No.10 (Fives Court). Outbuilding to the Old Parsonage (demolished 1862), extended as Racquets Court in 1850's, now house. Early 18th century and circa 1860. Diaper brick with flush quoins, pantiled roof. Main elevation facing south, single storey, raised circa 1860 to two storeys using reclaimed materials. Three bays, and attached to rear the racquets court, red brick, now part converted to dwelling. Central entrance, a boarded door in 20th century lean-to brick porch. Stone cross windows to ground floor with gauged brick lintels. Moulded two-light stone windows set into raised upper floor and roof extended as lean-to on court. Court is of four brick panels, two storeys, with nine and 12-paned sashes, and windows new in circa 1945.

No.11 (The Old House). Manor house. Recent re-examination of the roof-timbers shows a style and simplicity of construction suggesting an earlier date (1260-1290) than estimated in the 1972 survey, below. The present thickness of the walls also suggests that the original may have been largely of wood, reinforced later with brick and stone. One of 29 aisled halls in England. Early 14th, 16th century, remodelled late 17th/early 18th century, and restored 1873. Roughcast stonework with some brick, originally with some timber framing. Tiled roofs. Two storeys, two bays with cross wing at south-west end, rebuilt as double range wing. Entrance within gabled porch of 1873 in angle with extended wing. Timber ovolo moulded 20th century windows with diamond pattern leaded glazing. The eastern range has two added further wings to east with a secondary entrance on north side. Numerous gables. Interior: the house contains an early medieval double-aisled open hall structure with contemporary cross-wing of two bays within a rectangular plan of stone walls. Half bay at north-east end probably contained cross passage, and

services possibly in a separate structure beyond, now absent. Sphere truss against passage and central truss of hall has large archbraces springing from outer walls to cambered collar between square set arcade plates. Crown post above with steep straight braces to upper collar and collar purlin. Trenches for former louvre near apex of rafters. Wall posts to stone wall dividing wing from hall. Roof over hall smoke-blackened. Similar crow post truss to centre of wing. Fireplace, probably 16th century, inserted into cross passage, stone with four-centred arch and rounded arris. Secondary stair at side. Main stair in extension of wing forward, late 17th/early 18th century, with turned balusters and heavy handrail, swept up at newels. Main drawing room in north-west corner, formerly the wing, has 17th century oak panelling and cornice, the ceiling divided by deep chamfered cross beams. Gable stacks. Centre dining room within former hall, has main fireplace, described above, and early 18th century panelled dado. Room behind stack now kitchen. Chamber over dining room has bolection moulded fireplace in stone. Some 17th century iron casement windows to first floor window, with quadrant stays and turnbuckles. The only known aisled hall in the county.

WHITE STREET
Nos.3 & 5. Early-mid 19th century. Ashlar limestone facing to greensand rubble. Slate roof. Two storeys, three bays. Left bay has late 19th century shopfront with glazed door and fascia on consoles. Centre bay. No.3. has half glazed door and right bay, cranked back following line of street, replaced flush door and rectangular decorative overlight. 12-paned sashes to upper floor. Cornice and parapet to rear, tall eight-paned sashes. Rear extension behind shop, roughcast and flat roof.

No.19 (Beech House). House set back from road. 17th century, altered 1725 and later. Rendered stonework with tiled roof. Two storeys to front, one plus storeys to rear, with cellar and attics. Four bays, Plan and floor levels much altered since 17th century. Central six-panelled door in wide portico. 18th century two-centred arched timber windows with "Y" tracery and intersecting leading. Right bay has 16-paned sashes. External stack added at front of second bay straddling window. Stair in front projection at left end. Single hipped dormer. Rear elevation partly raised to two storeys. One flat roofed dormer. Interior has stair hall with split stair formed in early 19th century and first floor raised. Ground floor to right bay lowered over cellar. The ground floor facing west is remarkable in that it shelves onto the hillside behind, so the ground is level with the first floor at the rear. A tunnel separates the earth bank from the house proper - an early and apparently effective method of preventing the intrusion of damp. The house also has unusually detailed documentation on its origins. The Gye family restored the south end of what must then have been a farmhouse in 1727 and there is a list of owners since 1787. The families of Welch and Gye, related through marriage, have owned it since 1887.

No.25 (Broadwell Leigh). House gable on to road. Mid-16th/17th century. Timber framed with wattle and daub infill. Thatched roof. Single storey and attic, five bays, comprising a two-bay core with lateral stack, now subdivided, and a chamber to rear, now dining room, with 19th century inserted stack. Further extensions, probably 19th century, containing kitchen and service rooms, and rebuild of gable end against street forming a subdivision of main hall, to form a study with independent entry and stack. Boarded doors with pent roofs. Original structure has small square framing to upper floor, the rear bay framing partly replaced in brick. Timber casement windows and rebuilt end against road has lean-to roof and paned windows. Interior claimed to have cruck truss between hall and inner bay, now interrupted by 19th century stack. Original cross beam to hall has bar and octagon chamfer stops, but simple chamfer on upper floor. Lateral fireplace blocked by partition between hall and study under cross beam with scoop and check stops.

No.10 (The Malthouse). 18th century. Colourwashed brick with pantiled roof. Two storeys, three bays. Entrance at right side. 16-paned sashes with timber lintels, two replaced on ground floor. Roof hipped to right. Included primarily for group value.

No.12. Later 18th century. Colourwashed brick with pantiled roof. Two storeys, three bays. Off centre six-panelled door with flat canopy on cut brackets. 16-paned sashes with flush boxes, but ground floor left window early 19th century in rebates with segmental head. Gable stack to left.

No.14 (Broadwell House). Early 19th century. Flemish brickwork, incorporating stone gable of earlier greensand structure raised in clunch. Slate roof. Two storeys, three bays, two rooms deep. Through stair hall plan with flanking reception rooms. Central six-panelled door with fanlight, over three steps and within arched recess. 16-paned sash windows with gauged lintels and keystones. Plat band. Wide boxed eaves and roof hipped. Stacks at sides. Single storey extensions on left with similar door.

Barn (to the north of Knapp Farmhouse). Late 18th century. Timber framed, faced on east and gables in brick. English garden wall bond. Pantiled roof. Framing weatherboarded on high brick sills. Nine bays, with midstreys in bays three and six, and lean-to additions between. Wall framing of wide spaced posts and straight tension braces. Roof has king post, tied beam trusses; braces to jowled wall posts. Double tier of purlins. Ninth bay divided by brick wall of half height.

No.26 (Knapp Farmhouse). Early/Mid 18th century. Brick in Flemish bond with stone quoins and dressings, tiled roofs. Two storeys, cellar and attics. "L"-plan with mid-19th century block in re-entrant angle. Through hall plan with lateral stair and parlours at ends, services in rear wing. West facade of 5 bays. Central entrance, a cross boarded door faced early 19th century with panelled frame, within stone bead arrised surround and stone flat canopy on brackets. Inserted stone segmental fanlight over. Plat band. Similar stone surrounds with flat entablature to 12-paned sash windows. Moulded stone eaves. Two-light earlier 18th century gable windows to attic with iron leaded casements. Two hipped dormers to attic. External stacks at rear of main rooms. Rear wing on left, single storey and attic, raised to two storeys, four bays, with three segmental headed windows and early 18th century sash in fourth bay. Early 19th century 12-pane casements to south side of wing and gable. Interior: Mid-19th century fireplaces, but large blocked fireplace in left parlour, perhaps the original kitchen. Large fireplace, also blocked, in rear wing, probably an addition. Moulded muntin panelling in attic landing. Double butt purlin roof. Segmental brick vaulted cellar for full length of main block. The building has a raised terrace to the farmyard on north side with a brick parapet and weathered stone coping.

RUSSELL MILL LANE
Russell Mill House. 18th century. Refronted late 18th/early 19th century. English garden wall bond, 20th century tiled roof. Two storeys and attics, three bays. Left bay and return along road remains from the earlier structure, and incorporated in new approximately symmetrical facade. Central stair hall plan with flanking reception rooms. Six-panelled door and fanlight in round arched opening. 16-paned sashes, renewed, and gauged brick lintels. Brick dentilled eaves. External gable stacks. Roof hipped, with two rebuilt gabled dormers. Wing on left has stair, three-storey quarter hipped to rear extended in 19th century.

EDGE OF THE VILLAGE
Clyffe Hall. House built in 1732, for Henry Vince II, early 19th century wings added, remodelled 1899 (date on rainwater heads) for E.C. Schomberg, east wing further extended 1905-10 possibly by C.E. Ponting and front and interiors altered circa 1904 by Ernest Newton. Roughcast, with rendered raised quoins, Bath stone details and slate roofs. Central block three storeys, attics and cellars. Double pile plan with internal stacks and stair in north-west corner. Original entrance said to be from south, altered to north circa 1904. Five bays, cornice and pediment. Central entrance, an oak six-panelled door with side and overlights within four-style Ionic portico. Tripartite window over and oval window in aedicule cresting. 12-paned sash windows. Wings to

right of two bays containing drawing room, to left also of two bays, extended in similar style by further two bays and forward terminal block containing kitchens, extended to rear as billiard room. Balustraded parapet for first two bays either side. Rear elevation has giant Corinthian pilasters and egg and dart cornice. Central Ionic portico. Roof hipped with many tall chimneys. Interior: Hall within central block has heavy oak panelling. Dog leg stair also of oak, 17th century design. Drawing room has timber overmantle to acanthus fire surround, and plaster ceiling. Lounge on south side has heavily dentilled cornice

Jeanne House. Large house, 1862 - 1869, built by Ewan Christian for Edward Pleydell Bouverie, now junior boarding house for Dauntsey's School. Red brick, with blue brick patterning and stone dressings. Slate roof. Two storeys and attic. Main block of three bays with link to large service block, itself linked to stables and carriage houses forming courtyard to north-east. Elizabethan revival style evolved from the domestic gothic of Pearson and Daukes. Imposing asymmetrical entrance on north side leading indirectly to large central hall. Porch has strapwork pilasters, dentilled cornice and blind traceried parapet, arched at centre and ball finials at corners. Arched opening over four steps. Cable over has initials E.P.B. and date 1865. Hall, on left has lettered parapet reading PATRIA CARA CARIOR LIBERTAS. Mullioned and transomed windows throughout, bay windows and canted bays, some with round arch to central two lights of four. Bays gabled, with stone kneelers and copings. Chimneys octagonal, of brick, moulded with letter B and strapwork, and have offsetting tops. Coats of arms in gables. Service block has central corridor and south front a five-bay round arched arcade stopping at tall clock tower with ogee lead roof and ball finial. Arcade continues beyond for four bays terminating in a three-bay arcaded gable. Stable and carriage yard in similar style, single storey with attics, gabled, enclosing a paved yard, and with stone gate pier at entrance. Interior: entrance lobby with fireplace, leads left to two-storey single aisled main hall, the arcade having polished marble columns and carved stone capitals supporting depressed two-centred arches. Tiled floor to aisle. Columned stone fireplace with entablature and scrolled fascia. First floor balcony cantilevered. Stair at south-west end, behind entrance lobby, timber, open well, with twisted balusters. Stained glass window to stair with owner's initials. Architect's panel under, reading "E. Christian, 1865. Contractor Futcher and Bentliff." Games room in south-east corner, carved stained pine overmantel, marble slips and encaustic tiles to fireplace. Ceiling with moulded ribs forming polygons. The refectory in south-west corner has a similar fireplace, with a tiled interior, and another, contemporary, with coloured marbles between these two rooms.

HOUSING ESTATES

Wiltshire County Council first built housing in Market Lavington in 1924 and estates have been added through the remainder of the century. The Alban estate at the Spring was added in 1928, followed in the 1930's by further developments on both sides of Spin Hill and at Northbrook. Since the Second World War more council houses have been built at the foot of Lavington Hill and others added to the estate at Northbrook. Since 1970 private developers have built new estates in Bouverie Drive, Canada Rise and, most recently at Grove Farm and again at Northbrook and Council policy points to continuing expansion.

WILDLIFE

The presence of the British Army on Salisbury Plain for more than a hundred years has been a boon for wildlife. The wild boar and the wolves disappeared in earlier centuries, but today the vast stretches of downland are assured retreats for the foxes, squirrels, fallow deer, rabbits, weasels, hedgehogs and badgers hunted elsewhere.

Vanished also from the fields around Market Lavington are exotic additions to the diets of past centuries, but these too can be found occasionally on the Plain. The Earl of Abingdon, the owner of Lavington manor two hundred years ago, reported that he ate, and sent to friends in London, morels, described as a type of large honeycomb-shaped mushroom. Bishop Tanner, whose father was for decades a vicar in the parish, reported that wild oats were a dietary supplement to the barley growing in the Clays.

The Army's occupation of the great grasslands on the Plain has also protected some of the rarer of the more than 80 species of birds in the area. Winter is probably the busiest time with flocks of fieldfares, redwings and thrushes in the fields and open country of the Plain. Individuals encountered on the Plain include skylarks and meadow pipits and lower down and often dangerously close to an early death on the roads are the pheasants and partridges. Then there are the ground-feeders like linnets, corn buntings, greenfinches, chaffinches and hedge sparrows, as well as goldfinches and goldcrests in the trees.

A very early harbinger of spring is the chiffchaff, who arrives from the south in March. Spring also sees departures when large flocks of fieldfares and redwings fly off to Scandinavia and the Baltic. Other species pair off and establish themselves in their own territory for the warmer months.

Summer is the time of the singers like warblers, and the eaves of the village houses are roosts for swallows, swifts and housemartins. Near the streams are the willow and marsh tits, and in the woodlands are the great, blue and long-tailed tits. The trees also are nesting places for the three varieties of woodpecker and for the nuthatches and treecreepers.

Add to this list the jackdaws, magpies, turtle doves, jays, bullfinches, blackbirds, robins, wrens, mistle thrushes and the occasional cuckoo, and the woodlands are teeming by July. Then there are the scavengers, the seagulls, and preying from above on most of this huge population are the sparrow hawks, kestrels and, also, buzzards. Bustards have been rare this century but seven were killed near the village in 1871. Theory had it that they were refugees from the gunfire in the Franco-Prussian war. They were later commemorated for a while by the Bustard Inn, on the old road across the Plain.

Open water supports the swans, moorhens, dabchicks, teal, tufted ducks and mallards, while an occasional lordly heron makes a visit to a quiet stream. Nightingales sometimes sing near Dewey's Water and in the sunken lanes.

As wild as any of these are the flowers of the grasslands, preserved as a by-product of the Army's occupation of the Plain. There are the lovely violets, the kidney vetch, sanfoin, toadflax, salad burnet, corn gromwell, scarlet pimpernel, cowslip and milkwort, and yellow ragwort is on the increase, interspersed with the purple of knapweed and the blue of scabius. Undoubtedly the most interesting flowers of the chalk uplands are the purple and spotted orchids, and the much rarer twayblade and the bee orchid.

Down from the Plain are common companions of any summer: daisies, poppies, chickweed, cowslips, primroses, hedge parsley, dandelions, ragged robin, cranesbill, potentillas, ladies' smock, buttercups, coltsfoot and groundsel. In the deeper woods, growing in the leaf mould, are the primroses, violets, bluebells, wood anemones, forget-me-nots, honeysuckle, wildrose and rosebay willow herb, interspersed occasionally by snowdrops, lesser celandine and wood sorrel.

BIBLIOGRAPHY

Annals Of Devizes, Part 1.

Atley, Rev. H. *A Topographical Account Of Market Lavington.* (1855)

Aubrey, John. *Wiltshire.* (1659-70)

Barber, Richard. *The Knight And Chivalry.* (1970)

Census returns.

Chambers, Jill. *Wiltshire Machine Breakers.* (1993)

Curl, James. *The Victorian Celebration Of Death. (*1972)

Defoe, Daniel. *A Tour Through The Whole Island Of Great Britain.* (1724)

Devizes Gazette, The.

Devizes Museum. Various documents and publications.

Dictionary Of National Biography, The.

Evans, G.E. *Pastoral Pedigree.* (1977)

Feiling Keith: *A History Of England* (1950)

Heaton, Herbert. *The Yorkshire Woollen And Worsted Industries.* (1920)

Historic Monuments Commission. *Registry Of Listed Houses.*

Horn, Pamela. *Rural Life In England In The First World War.* (1984)

Hoskins, W.G. *The Making Of The English Landscape.* (1955)

Jackson, John Edward. *Footnote To Aubrey.* (1862)

Journal Of The Movement Of The Regiment Of The Wilts Militia
        Commanded By Colonel Wyndham During Monmouth's Rebellion.

Kee, Robert. *The Green Flag: A History Of Irish Nationalism.* (1972)

McKisack, May. *The Fourteenth Century.* (1959)

Market Lavington Museum. Various documents.

Market Lavington Women's Institute scrapbooks.

Quarter Sessions Records of the 17th Century.

Radnor, Helen: Countess Dowager. *From A Great-Grandmother's Armchair.* (1927)

Saunders, Anne. *Russell Mill.* (1881)

Slocombe, Pamela. *Mediaeval Houses Of Wiltshire.*

Symonds, Richard. *Diary Of The Marches Of The Royal Army During The Great Civil War.*
        (British Museum Ms.)

Taswell-Langmead. *English Constitutional History.* (1919)

The Maroon Square: A History Of The 4th Battalion The Wiltshire Regiment.

Underdown, David. *Revel, Riot And Rebellion.* (1985-1988)

Underdown, David. *Clubmen Of The Civil War* - from *Past And Present.*

Victoria County History Of Wiltshire.

Watkin, Bruce. *A History Of Wiltshire.* (1989)

Waylen. *Wiltshire During The Civil War.*

Weekly Dispatch, The.

Welch, James F. *Notes On Market Lavington.* (1953)

Wiltshire Archaeological & Natural History Magazine, The.

Wiltshire Independent, The.

Wiltshire Local Studies Library, Trowbridge. Various publications.

Wiltshire Notes And Queries.

Wiltshire Records Office, Trowbridge. Various documents.

Wiltshire Records Society: *The Notebooks Of William Hunt, Magistrate.*

Wiltshire Records Society: *The Edington Cartulary.* (Janet H. Stevenson Ed.)

Wiltshire Records Society: *Tradesmen In Early Stuart Wiltshire.* (J.J.Williams)

Wiltshire Records Society: *List Of Taxpayers For The Subsidy Of 1576.*

Wiltshire Records Society: *The Benevolence Of 1545.*

Wiltshire Times & News, The.

INDEX

Page numbers in italics refer to illustrations